GW00542011

Education and its Disciplines

Education
and its Disciplines

edited by R. G. Woods

University of London Press Ltd

ISBN 0 340 15985 5 Boards
ISBN 0 340 15986 3 Unibook

Copyright © 1972 R. G. Woods, M. V. J. Seaborne,
W. S. Anthony, G. Bernbaum

All rights reserved. No part of this publication
may be reproduced or transmitted in any form or
by any means, electronic or mechanical, including
photocopy, recording, or any information storage
and retrieval system, without permission in
writing from the publisher.

University of London Press Ltd
St Paul's House, Warwick Lane, London EC4P 4AH

Printed in Great Britain by
T. & A. Constable Ltd
Hopetoun Street, Edinburgh EH7 4NF

Foreword

The setting up of a new structure for the Diploma in Educational Studies at the University of Leicester School of Education in September 1971 provided an appropriate occasion to arrange a short series of lectures designed to introduce the four supporting educational disciplines and to demonstrate that rigour and relevance are not necessarily polarised. The lectures, which now appear in this volume, were prepared and delivered by four of my colleagues at Leicester, each of whom sees the 'basic' disciplines as central to the study of education. It is hoped that the book will contribute usefully to the dialogue between students and staff in colleges and departments of education about the aptness of their courses.

Leicester 1971   *John F. Kerr*

Contents

Introduction
Ronald Woods

In the papers which follow, four main disciplines – philosophy, history, psychology and sociology – are singled out as having particular reference to educational problems. Their concern is with *educational* problems and this is marked by referring to 'history of education', 'philosophy of education', and so on, but it should be noted that there do not exist the disciplines of philosophy, history, psychology and sociology *and* the quite separate and distinct disciplines of philosophy of education, history of education, and the rest. Support for this view is to be found in the contributions themselves, in which the writers relate their studies in each case to the parent discipline. An adequate characterisation of the nature of psychology of education, for example, demands a characterisation of the nature of psychology itself.

Why does one have to contend with four disciplines when studying education? Why not simply study the discipline of education? The short answer to this is that education is not a discipline. There are educational problems varying considerably in scope and complexity, but there is no set of specifically educational techniques and procedures with which to tackle these problems. It is necessary to have recourse to one or more of the underlying disciplines. If one is enquiring into the rôle and function of head teachers, how can sociology be avoided? If the enquiry is into how the age of eleven came to be associated with the transition from primary to secondary schooling, how can history be avoided? If investigating the nature, point and purpose of intelligence quotients, how can psychology be avoided? If the concern is to lay down a curriculum for, say, general secondary education, how can philosophy be avoided? No doubt these sorts of considerations were in the mind of R. F. Dearden when he wrote:

> In fact, I do not know quite what an 'educationist' is, or what sort of expert or authority he is supposed to be. I

know what a philosopher of education is, or an educational
psychologist or an educational sociologist, but I am not at
all sure what a plain 'educationist' would be.[1]

It may be that one would not wish to go quite as far as Dearden.
The term 'educationist' does have, or can be given, meaning.
An educationist is, or ought to be, a person well versed in the
four supporting disciplines who brings them to bear appro-
priately on questions relating to education. Whether there
could ever be such a person is a debatable issue. R. S. Peters
doubts that there could:

> To train people in even two such disciplines at once is
> quite an undertaking. I have experience of this; for my
> job at the University of London is to train people for the
> joint degree in Philosophy and Psychology, which in-
> volves at least a three-year course in the central problems
> of both these disciplines. Even these closely linked dis-
> ciplines are concerned with such different types of problem
> and employ such different types of procedure for answer-
> ing them that only very able students can gain some sort of
> mastery of both these disciplines. Yet what other discip-
> lines are more central to education than these? To con-
> template subsuming, not just these two disciplines, but
> also history and sociology under a general discipline of
> education not only seems to be logically absurd; it is also,
> I should say, practically impossible.[2]

Whatever the answer to the empirical question as to whether
there exists, or will exist, a polymathic educationist one thing,
at least, is clear: such an educationist would necessarily employ
a number of distinct skills and procedures, for there is certainly
no discipline of education for him to practise. The mistaken
belief that there is such a discipline is partly responsible for
the poverty-stricken nature of courses in 'Principles of Education' and for the plethora of 'educational' writings lacking all
identity.

These remarks are strictly relevant to a matter raised by
Malcolm Seaborne at the end of his paper and referred to

both by Gerald Bernbaum and in my own paper on philosophy of education – the matter of integration. It is sometimes contended that courses on education based upon a 'distinct disciplines' approach lack coherence and unity – the philosopher, historian, sociologist and psychologist each go their separate ways and no attempt is made to 'integrate' or 'synthesise' their respective approaches. The implication here is that some kind of combination of logically distinct statements gives rise to yet a further type of statement, the genuine, *bona fide* educational statement. The educational disciplines lose their identity in the one overriding discipline of education, and in this way unity arises out of diversity. In this extreme form the argument, in line with what has already been said in this introduction, is untenable. The most that can be said is that it serves to remind us that education courses might be improved if the specialists in the underlying disciplines had regard for what was going on in other components of those courses. This might lead to a conscious attempt to deal with common topics, to the organisation of joint seminars, and so on. Not only students but also their teachers might well benefit from this. It can be no bad thing for a philosopher to hear at first-hand his colleague in psychology explicate the concept of motivation, just as there seems to be no good reason why representatives of all four specialisms should not conduct a joint examination of the justification, or lack of justification, for, say, comprehensive systems of education. To this extent, and to this extent only, pleas for integration make sense.

Part of the rationale behind the demand for integrated courses or for interdisciplinary enquiry consists in asserting that 'Life is One' or 'Life is Whole' and that distortion results if *aspects* of 'Life' are singled out for study. I do not wish here to analyse the confusion and errors inherent in this view, but simply to remark that the notion of relevance arises often in the context of slogans of the type 'Education is for Life'. Thus, to a student training to be a teacher it may well be that problems of discipline and control bulk large on teaching practice. Without a doubt these problems are part of the student's life and any theoretical studies not directly geared to their solution are then characterised as 'not relevant'. Theoretical studies ought to be related to life, so runs the argument, and hence, within the particular context under scrutiny, ought to contain prescriptions relating to the control of recalcitrant school children. If they do not contain prescriptions telling students what they ought to do in defined classroom situations then they are worthless because 'not relevant'. Without prejudice to the question as to whether theoretical studies *do* have a bearing on such eminently practical issues, one point is clear: there is a serious danger that in combining the study of education through its disciplines with teacher training conceived of in a narrow sense, we shall end up with emasculated academic courses of the 'tips for teachers' variety.

The solution to this problem seems to me to be essentially an organisational one. The disciplined study of education must be conducted at a time when and in an atmosphere in which teachers, or intending teachers, are relatively free from the pressures of immediate classroom concerns. Thus, as far as universities and their departments of education are concerned, educational studies ought to figure, as is already the case in some of the new universities, in undergraduate courses. There need be no commitment to teaching as a career on the part of those undertaking such courses. Students who subsequently elect to teach will then be divisible broadly into two classes – those who have and those who have not engaged in undergraduate educational studies. Differential treatment of these two classes will then be required at postgraduate level. The one-year course of training leading to the award of the postgraduate certificate of education will need to be extended to two years by making full use of the probationary year. The first of these two years could then be devoted to educational studies on the part of students who did not undertake them at undergraduate level and the second year would be concerned with school-based method work making use of the teacher-tutor system. Students of education at undergraduate level might well pass directly to this second year. For colleges of education, rather more radical reconstruction may be required. Perhaps it is that they should move towards a liberal arts college pattern in which courses are structured along university lines. This would be to depart from the conception of colleges as institutions catering solely for intending teachers and would, so far as the study of education is concerned, enable organisation similar to that suggested for universities to be implemented. Finally, there is the question of provision for established serving teachers. Unlike their younger colleagues in training, serving teachers of some standing will not in general find themselves dominated by immediate classroom pressures and to this extent will not push the 'relevance' argument mentioned above to absurd extremes. Provision of opportunity for them to engage in disciplined educational study may therefore be offered on a part-time basis although it is to be hoped that an increase in the budget for in-service education would enable them to be seconded to full-time courses leading to the award of diplomas, B.Eds, and M.Eds.

Detailed remarks on my part as to what the papers in this volume are about are not called for. An attempt was made to establish some degree of uniformity of treatment by suggesting that the contributors address themselves to three main questions: the nature of the discipline involved, the justification for its study, and the way or ways in which it ought to be taught. In general the contributors have adhered to this outline plan. Beyond this, however, they have developed their detailed arguments within the limitations imposed by the nature of the discipline concerned. Positive suggestions emerge relating to course content, ways of presenting that content, and so on. Additionally, and perhaps more importantly, a degree of consensus is achieved as to what the rôle of the educational disciplines should be. Seaborne's remark that more is required of the teacher than 'pedagogical expertise', Anthony's advocacy of a 'reason-oriented' approach, Bernbaum's quotation from Burns ('The practice of sociology is criticism'), my own stress on the eminently critical nature of analytic philosophy – all these point towards the disciplines as being seen as something more than a repository of useful pieces of information about teaching. The 'something more' is related to education in a broad sense and has much to do with the notion of transforming people into critical thinkers. As Conant observes:

> School people are under incessant pressure from ideological, economic, political, and other social groups to mould the schools in their interests. An understanding of the values of such groups as they bear on educational practice seems an important part of the equipment with which teachers should be provided. Skill in the analysis of propositions used in these debates is also of value. To develop this understanding and skill, rather than, as is often attempted, to produce by indoctrination partisans of a particular point of view, should be the aim of the college or university.[3]

References

1   Dearden, R. F., 'Philosophy and the curriculum', in *Curriculum Development*, Themes in Education No. 21, Conference Report. University of Exeter Institute of Education, 1970, p. 2.

2   Peters, R. S., 'Comments on J. Walton's paper "A discipline of education" ' in Walton, J. and Kuethe, J. L. (ed.), *The Discipline of Education*, Madison, Wis., University of Wisconsin Press, 1963, pp. 18-19.

3   Conant, J. B., *The Education of American Teachers*. New York, McGraw-Hill, 1963, p. 121. Quoted by Taylor, W., *Society and the Education of Teachers*, Faber and Faber, 1969, p. 121.

Philosophy of Education

Ronald Woods

WHAT IS PHILOSOPHY OF EDUCATION?

In this first section I shall argue essentially for a conception of philosophy of education in which it is seen as a branch of philosophy in general, not as a study or discipline in its own right in the sense that the modes of argument, techniques of analysis and the like are in some way peculiar to that study. It follows that characterisation of the nature of philosophy of education demands characterisation of the nature of philosophy itself.

All the world seems to have *some* conception of philosophy and of the philosopher. One prevalent popular conception of the philosopher sees him as a grey-bearded sage possessed of infinite wisdom, the man to whom people look to tell them, for example, how they might so order their affairs on this planet as to ensure everlasting peace and harmony, how individuals should regulate their lives if they would achieve satisfaction, or happiness, or a sense of fulfilment. On occasions individuals themselves assume this philosophic rôle and mark the fact by prefacing observations on, say, how they view life with the phrase, 'My philosophy of life is . . .', or 'In my more philosophic moments I sometimes think that . . .' The dispute as to whether this kind of popular, do-it-yourself philosophy, consisting for the most part of isolated saws, aphorisms or proverbs, is at all deserving of the name 'philosophy' is a somewhat barren one. Perhaps of more profit in this connection is to attempt to see why such aphorisms tend to be called 'philosophical' in everyday speech rather than to wrangle over the rather fine linguistic point as to whether in fact they merit this tag. What are the resemblances, if any, between popular philosophising and other kinds of philosophising? And what, if any, are the dissimilarities?

There are three basic features that popular philosophy seems to possess, or that people who engage in it seem to want to stress. The first is some degree of generality. The popular philosopher seems to be trying to arrive at a concise verbal summary of past experience, a pithy statement of what 'life' is all about. Often the concise verbal summary is meant not simply to sum up 'life' but also to act as a guide to future action. Without doubt an important strand in the popular conception of the philosopher is related to this second notion, that of action – the philosopher is a man who can tell us what to *do*, or who can tell us what beliefs we ought to hold, these beliefs being of a kind that relate directly to what we ought to do. One of the recurring criticisms of professional philosophers consists precisely in charging them with failure to provide guides to action; as philosophers they ought, it is popularly felt, to see it as one of their foremost tasks to make practical pronouncements. And when they fail to do so, they are unworthy of being called 'philosophers', and, more seriously, the discipline they study is not worth bothering with. A third concern of popular philosophy, not unconnected with the notion of generality, consists in attempts on the part of its practitioners to get to the heart of things; there is concern with fundamental or essential matters.

There may be other features possessed by popular philosophy, but it seems to me that these three point to the reason why popular philosophy gets to be called 'philosophy' at all. This is because the features in question are possessed also by philosophy of another kind, the more stringent and intellectually demanding kind as practised over the centuries. Bertrand Russell characterised this second kind of philosophy, which I shall call 'traditional' philosophy, in terms of the sorts of questions with which it was concerned:

Is the world divided into mind and matter, and, if so, what is mind and what is matter? Is mind subject to matter, or is it possessed of independent powers? Has the universe any unity or purpose? Is it evolving towards some goal? Are there really laws of nature, or do we believe in them only because of our innate love of order? Is man what he seems to the astronomer, a tiny lump of impure carbon and water impotently crawling on a small and unimportant planet? Or is he what he appears to Hamlet? Is he perhaps both at once? Is there a way of living that is noble, in what does it consist, and how shall we achieve it? Must the good be eternal in order to deserve to be valued, or is it worth seeking even if the universe is inexorably moving towards death? Is there such a thing as wisdom, or is what seems such merely the ultimate refinement of folly?[1]

But while there can be seen in these questions, and in the attempts to answer them, concern for generality, fundamentality and action, and hence a link can be established between traditional and popular philosophy, there can also be seen ways in which these two types of philosophy differ from one another. The salient difference between them lies, surely, in the fact that the popular variety lacks depth and is essentially superficial in that little in the way of sustained thinking or analysis precedes the conclusions arrived at. Indeed, very often the 'conclusions' consist of no more than some statement or other made as a result of immediate emotional pressures. On the other hand, consideration of traditional philosophy reveals that this is an altogether more rigorous affair, engaged in systematically over long periods of time by men of commanding intellectual stature. Lengthy, painstaking reflective thinking is the order of the day in this field and it is not open to just anybody, as is the case with popular philosophy, to engage in

B

this kind of philosophical discourse without having served a somewhat arduous apprenticeship.

However, given the superiority of traditional over popular philosophy, it does not follow that traditional philosophy is free from defect. One seemingly mundane, and yet important, defect attributed to it by some philosophers consists in the difficulty of understanding much of it. The writings of a number of traditional philosophers, such as Spinoza, Hegel, Bergson, Bradley, pose grave difficulties of understanding and these difficulties are not simply a function of the intelligence, or lack of it, on the part of those studying these writers. Thus, R. S. Peters relates this anecdote:

> One of my most sobering experiences in teaching was the first time I lectured on Hegel – a philosopher whom I confess I have never properly understood. On that occasion I understood almost nothing about what he was getting at – yet afterwards I was congratulated by one or two students on giving a brilliant lecture![2]

That the difficulty of understanding referred to is not simply a function of the intelligence of the student comes out quite clearly in A. J. Ayer's *Language, Truth and Logic* which appeared in 1936. Ayer, in what today would be regarded as a rather rough-and-ready fashion, divided all statements, or propositions, into two classes, the class of analytic statements which are, crudely speaking, true or false by definition (for example, 'a quadruped is a four-footed animal', 'a bachelor is an unmarried man'), and the class of synthetic, or empirical, statements the truth or falsity of which is determined by some possible sense-experience (for example, 'Big Ben is in London', 'The moon is made of cheese'). For Ayer analytic and synthetic statements are, or at least were, the only sorts of statements there are. If a putative statement fails to satisfy the sense-experience test appropriate to empirical statements, and if it is not analytic, then, says Ayer, 'I hold that it is metaphysical, and that, being metaphysical, it is neither true nor false, but literally senseless.' And he continues:

It will be found that much of what ordinarily passes for philosophy is metaphysical according to this criterion, and, in particular, that it can not be significantly asserted that there is a non-empirical world of values, or that men have immortal souls, or that there is a transcendent God.[3]

We see then that the difficulty of understanding much traditional philosophy most certainly is not, in Ayer's view, to be attributed to obtuseness on the part of the reader; it is simply the case that there is nothing to understand! It is important to note the stress on the concept of understanding. Given that very few practising philosophers today would endorse Ayer's account of two classes of statement, nevertheless many of them would accept that his stress, albeit implied, on the importance of understanding what is said was right, that it makes good sense to pose with respect to a philosophical assertion the twin questions, 'What does it mean?' and 'What sort of evidence would back up the assertion assuming that one could ferret out its meaning?' Indeed, these twin questions might well serve to identify a third kind of philosophy in which the accent is on the clarification and critical evaluation of ideas, on meaning, and on the uncovering of presupposition and assumption. This kind of philosophy is often referred to these days as 'analytic' philosophy. Of the types of philosophy so far considered this seems to me to be the most rewarding and fruitful, and hence most deserving of the title of 'philosophy'. One of the reasons – perhaps the principal reason – why I consider it rewarding and fruitful lies simply in that its practitioners are intent on seeing that genuine communication takes place between disputants by diligent questioning designed to ensure that each disputant understands, to the fullest possible extent, what others are saying. And this seems to me to be a simple good. Too much talking and writing about education, for example, is vitiated by a lack of concern for clarity, and yet clarity is a prerequisite for subsequent critical evaluation. To take one example. In a book concerned with curriculum matters the authors thought that it would be a good idea – and it *is* a good idea – to 'lay bare some of [their] assumptions about *persons, education, schooling,* and *curriculum*'. This they proceeded to do as follows:

> Our commitment is to man as a person. A person is a being with consciousness and intelligence, equally able to be conscious of self and others. He is emancipated from simple location; he is related to others not merely by contact but by contemplation. He is able to entertain purposes and appreciate values. As an agent or actor he is capable not only of apprehending truth but of doing the truth. As a spiritual whole he is stubbornly indissoluble by scientific analysis and unsubmergible in any universal essence. The person *is* reality. He is free and morally responsible. He is an end not a means. The person in man is what the doctrines of equality refer to, the medium of understanding, the source of language, and the explanation of love.[4]

Now, here, if one follows the analytic course, one needs to ask questions like, 'What does it mean to "do the truth"?' If you, the reader, were asked, 'Have you done any truths lately?', what would your reaction be? Would you immediately understand what you were being asked and be able to answer? Again, what are the universal essences in which man cannot be submerged? What is the point of stressing that the person *is* reality? In what sense is man free? What is he free from? What is he free to do? In posing these questions I am not trying to suggest that man *isn't* any of the things that King and Brownell say that he is, or that he possesses none of the characteristics that they say he possesses. My object is the essentially uncomplicated one of attempting to understand their assertions, to find out what they mean so that I am able to pass to a consideration of the truth or falsity of those assertions, that is, to the stage of critical evaluation.

Philosophy as analysis, then, is very much concerned with meaning.[5] Hence the phrase 'linguistic analysis' (often used these days) to bring out this concern with meaning and to disabuse those who might think that philosophical analysis is akin, say, to chemical analysis. Analytic philosophers do not take very careful looks at chairs in order to penetrate to the very heart of 'chairness', nor do they experiment with chairs to this end. They are not empirical scientists engaged in trying to get fresh information about things in the world, nor are they super-scientists engaged in attempting to ascertain just what is the nature of the ultimate stuff of the universe.

It is of importance to note that the third kind of philosophy is concerned with meaning in a wide sense and not solely in the comparatively restricted sense of producing verbal equivalents (as when we say that 'quadruped' means 'four-footed animal'). Meaning in a wider sense is connected, for example, with observations regarding the reasons for particular statements being made. Language is not used *solely* to describe, to state facts. When a mother says, 'The party's over, children', it might be to the point to observe that she is not intent on stating the fact that the party is over, but intent on getting these noisy children out of her house. Some time ago Jennie Lee said that the debate about comprehensive schools was over. She used fact-stating language – 'The debate about comprehensive schools is over' – but surely only the naïve would suppose that she was stating a fact. Was not the whole point of her remark, it could be argued, to steam-roller some people into acceptance of comprehensive schemes of education? Meaning, then, in *this* particular wider sense, is bound up with the notion of what people want to do, want to bring about by their use of language.

To continue the exploration of meaning we must note the importance of the concept of the emotive use of language. If A calls B a swine, it is manifest that B is not a swine in the literal sense of that term but that A is, maybe, using this expression as a means of giving vent to his hostile feelings towards B, as a means of getting other people to see B in a most unfavourable light, and so on. Some philosophers have argued convincingly that as far as some emotively charged words are concerned ('good', for example), it is a waste of time looking for a verbal equivalent. The meaning of 'good' is elucidated not by trying to produce an equivalent but by observing that when someone says of a small boy that he is 'good' the word is not so much *describing* the boy (compare saying that the boy is pale) as *evaluating* the boy's behaviour in general, or a particular piece of behaviour, and finding in favour of it: praising the boy by saying that he is good. We can usefully oppose the concept of descriptive meaning to the concept of emotive meaning. To say that 'quadruped' means 'four-footed animal' is to proffer a descriptive definition; in general, the word 'quadruped' does not carry emotive overtones. Now some words contain an element of descriptive and an element of emotive meaning. Consider as an example the word 'profession'.[6] A reasonably accurate descriptive definition of this word would be 'an occupation or job, especially one that involves some branch of learning or science'. But there is more to the word than this. Whereas it would not be doing any class of creatures a favour or disfavour to apply the term 'quadruped' to them, and no class of creatures would take umbrage at the application, it might well be felt that a favour was being done to some group of people by applying the term 'profession' to them, or they might take it that a favour was being done them, because the word tends to carry favourable emotive overtones. There is the idea that professions are in some sense better than non-professions, that professions ought to receive privileged treatment. In short, 'profession' has emotive as well as descriptive content. Of great importance here, with particular reference to words possessing both descriptive and emotive meaning, is Charles L. Stevenson's account of 'persuasive definitions':

> In any 'persuasive definition' the term defined is a familiar one, whose meaning is both descriptive and strongly emotive. The purport of the definition is to alter the descriptive meaning of the term, usually by giving it greater precision within the boundaries of its customary vagueness; but the definition does *not* make any substantial

change in the term's emotive meaning. And the definition
is used, consciously or unconsciously, in an effort to
secure, by this interplay between emotive and descriptive
meaning, a redirection of people's attitudes.[7]

Thus, to consider the notion of a profession once more, suppose
a man wants to use the word 'profession' in such a way as to
include plumbing among the professions. An objection is
raised that the proposed usage violates prior usage of the word
'profession' in so far as prior usage tends to demand that for a
person to be a member of a profession he or she must engage
in a fairly prolonged period of academic study at an institution
such as a university. But this objection is ignored by the man
proposing the new definition – his object is to relax the prevailing descriptive definitional criteria in such a way that plumbing
satisfies *his* descriptive definitional criteria, his ultimate object
being to take advantage of the favourable emotive import of
the word 'profession' so that plumbing is accorded the sort of
treatment that has hitherto been accorded to callings such as
medicine and law. He wants people's attitudes towards plumbing to change and he reckons this will be brought about if, in
the future, plumbing is accorded the title of 'profession'.
Where the term being persuasively defined has no determinate
prior usage, where it possesses, in Stevenson's language,
'vagueness', then it may well be that the element of redefinition
involved in the whole process passes unnoticed. One further
point. We must note that *practical* issues are involved here. In
the plumbing example the central point at issue is: 'Ought
plumbers to be treated in ways in which professional people
are treated?' This is essentially a practical question raising the
issue of how classes of people are to be treated. In one sense
the dispute concerns words ('It's only a matter of words'), but
it would be dangerously short-sighted to suppose that disputes
concerning words have no practical effect. Indeed, the way in
which such disputes are related to practice is evident time and
time again in talk and writing about education, for in one
sense education is pre-eminently a practical activity and

educationists are very often concerned endlessly to debate the question, 'What ought to be done?' We ought not, then, to be surprised to find in educational writings numerous instances of the emotive or persuasive use of language, sometimes cleverly concealed, sometimes used unwittingly by the writer, sometimes blatant. We need to be aware of this dimension in the use of language. Without such awareness we could well find ourselves being hoodwinked into taking up a practical stance on an educational issue without really understanding what is actually involved. Without such awareness we could well find some educational writings inducing in us a sense of euphoria, a sense of generalised well-being, causing us to suspend disbelief and to postpone a long, hard, critical look at what positively is being said.

In remarking on the importance of the concept of meaning in philosophy I have referred more than once to the use of language. I would draw particular attention to this question of use. It is fundamentally incorrect to suppose that *every* word has a definite, distinct meaning which can be ascertained if only one searches diligently enough, if only sufficient time is allowed for contemplation. There is a strong temptation to think that words have a life of their own, that, with great cunning, they hide from human gaze their essential meaning and that only men possessed of almost superhuman insight can get at this meaning. Consider words like 'university', 'education', 'democracy', 'freedom', 'justice', 'truth', 'goodness', 'beauty', and so on. Philosophers through the ages have set themselves the task of attempting to establish what democracy *really* is, what beauty *really* is. Plato, in his *Republic*, sets Socrates on a prolonged search for the essential nature of justice. It is not difficult to see here the existence of the presupposition that there *is* a *thing* which *is* justice and which the word 'justice' names. Now, a number of contemporary philosophers have set their faces against this doctrine of essentialism, and argue, cogently to my mind, that prolonged contemplation and meditation aimed at exposing 'true' meaning is not the way to get at meaning at all, and that what we must do is look at the word, or words, under consideration in action, that is, in use. Thus we have Wittgenstein's dictum that the meaning of a word is its use. And very often the 'use' to which reference is made is what has come to be called 'ordinary use', that is, the use of language by 'ordinary', philosophically unself-conscious men and women as they go about their daily tasks. Certainly the appeal to ordinary use is an effective way of getting philosophical debate off the ground. Thus, to take a simple example, suppose someone of a sceptical turn of mind says, 'Nobody ever understands anybody else.' One way of getting clear about this remark (and until one is clear about it what can be said?) is to reply in this way: 'But people do in fact say things such as, "Although he spoke with a strong German accent, nevertheless I understood everything that he said." This is undeniably a correct use of the word "understood", so in saying that nobody ever understands anybody else you are either saying something that is false or you are using the word "understand" in a very special sense. What is this sense, please?' In this reply, note the appeal to the ordinary use of the word 'understand'; the implication here is that surely no one who speaks the English language, certainly no one whose native tongue is English, could possibly deny the fact that English speaking people do talk in the way the counter-example suggests that they do. And given that the sceptic cannot deny this fact it follows that in his remark, 'Nobody ever understands anybody else', he must be using 'understand' in a way that is not the way in which it is used in the counter-example. He is thus forced to specify more clearly just what it is that he is trying to convey in his statement. This will result in his making further statements which themselves can be tested for clarity in the way in which his first statement was tested, and the ultimate object will be to arrive at clear statements of which it can be asked, 'Are they true or false?'

Of course, appeals to ordinary usage are only legitimate when the statement under review is couched in everyday language, as in 'Nobody ever understands anybody else.' If our enquiry is into the meaning of the word 'force', occasioned, shall we say, by someone asserting that force is the product of mass and acceleration, then it would be extremely silly to embark on an examination of ordinary uses of the word 'force' (for example, 'He forced me to sign the statement') in order to get clear about and to check up on the truth or falsity of the statement. The proper place to look in order to check up on the meaning and the truth or falsity of *this* particular statement is, obviously, an elementary text-book on physics. To ascertain the meanings of some terms we need to have regard to the theories, of a more or less rigorous kind, in which these terms are used, and we shall often find that within these theories the terms have been relatively precisely defined. Again, there is nothing to stop someone using familiar words in outlandish ways provided he tells us how he is using them. Thus, in a sense, there is nothing to stop a man saying, 'A person is educated if and only if he can pass a camel through the eye of a needle.' We shall now know that, when he says of A that he is not educated, he means no more than that A is unable to pass a camel through the eye of a needle. We shall understand him although we shall try, no doubt, to persuade him that he is wrong to want to use the word 'educated' in such a strange way. But these kinds of reservations – technical language, eccentric private usage – apart, we shall invariably find a survey of the ordinary use of a term a valuable way of initiating philosophical enquiry.

One last point needs to be made about the concept of use in relation to the concepts of essentialism (in the sense of 'one, and only one, true meaning') and vagueness, although it is a reminder more than anything else. It is this. We must not suppose that examination of words in use will always result in our being able to offer absolutely precise definitions of those words or definitive lists of criteria governing their use. This is in accord with what has already been said about the doctrine of essentialism and links with the fact that the meanings of a number of words are vague. Thus, consider the word 'game'. What, we might ask, does this word *really* mean? What is the one feature denoted by this word and present in all things called 'games'? But if we do ask these questions we are surely mistaken in so doing, for as Wittgenstein observes in a celebrated passage in his *Philosophical Investigations*, a passage in which he is concerned to ascertain the features possessed in common by different games – card games, children's games, football, cricket, made-up games, and so on:

> What is common to them all? – Don't say: 'There *must* be something common, or they would not be called 'games' – but *look and see* whether there is anything common to all. – For if you look at them you will not see something that is common to *all*, but similarities, relationships, and a whole series of them at that. To repeat: don't think, but look![8]

And Wittgenstein coined the phrase 'family resemblances' to refer to the series of similarities and relationships. The connection between this notion of family resemblances and the notion of vagueness ought to be reasonably clear, and will serve once more to remind us that very often in philosophical enquiry the search for essential meanings is a fruitless one.

Very often the third kind of philosophy, referred to above as 'linguistic analysis', is referred to as 'conceptual analysis'. Now, taking as correct Professor Geach's assertion that 'The central and typical applications of the term "having a concept" are those in which a man is master of a bit of linguistic usage'[9] (to take one of Geach's examples, if someone knows how to use the English word 'red', then he has a concept of red) then clearly there is no significant difference in meaning between the phrase 'conceptual analysis' and the phrase 'linguistic analysis'. To put the matter another way, in practising conceptual analysis we seek to clarify and pin down the concepts which we use in understanding the world and in communicating our thoughts, but in communicating we make use above all of words and so concepts are clarified by the examination of our use of words. It follows that there is no significant difference between saying that analytic philosophy is concerned (partly) with the meaning of words and saying that it is concerned (partly) with concepts. Now consider the following list of concepts: electron, love, Tuesday, quadratic equation, lozenge, vector, philosophy, the pound sterling, breakfast, knowledge, consubstantiation, newspaper, refraction. In so far as philosophy is concerned with concepts, it would appear that one can philosophise about anything. In John Wisdom's words:

> Analytic philosophy has no special subject-matter. You can philosophise about Tuesday, the pound sterling, and lozenges and philosophy itself.[10]

But now let us look again at the above list of concepts and ask if it is possible to assign any of them to a specific department of knowledge or, to use a word currently favoured, to a specific discipline. It does seem that it is possible to do this. 'Electron' and 'refraction' belong to physics, 'quadratic equation' and 'vector' to mathematics, 'consubstantiation' to theology, and so on. We might then be led to surmise that concentration on the analysis of concepts employed in a particular discipline leads to the establishment of a particular branch of philosophy designated as 'the philosophy of' the discipline concerned. Thus, we have, as it were, specialisms within philosophy – philosophy of history, of mathematics, of science, of religion, and so on – linked or unified, however, by the fact that these specialisms are all concerned (partly) with conceptual analysis.

What I have been doing in the last paragraph is getting a little clearer about the meaning of the phrase 'conceptual analysis' and of the term 'concept'. We can now use this language to pose further questions. Thus, the physicist, say, is interested in the concepts of his discipline, and, this being so, how do we distinguish the physicist's interest from the philosopher's interest? In general terms the answer to this is that the physicist will *use* concepts and the theories expressed in terms of those concepts in order to continue his exploration of natural phenomena, and, of course, experiment will play an important part in this exploration. I shall say that the physicist is interested in first-order questions. The philosopher, on the other hand, is not interested in using physical concepts and theories in this way, nor is he concerned to conduct physical experiments; rather he speculates *about* the facts, concepts and theories of physicists. He may be interested in comparing the nature of scientific observation with ordinary everyday observation and this interest may lead him to consider the question of the reality of things like atoms, electrons, neutrons, and so on, which figure in the physicist's theoretical scheme, or he may be at pains to attempt to specify just what is involved when physicists 'explain' things. I shall say that the philosopher is interested in second-order questions. Note that when I talk of 'the physicist' and 'the philosopher' this way of talking is consonant with the fact that physicist and philosopher may be one and the same person undertaking different jobs at different times. There is nothing to stop a physicist reflecting about the nature of his concepts and theories; indeed, sometimes it is necessary that he do so in order that his first-order work can proceed:

> Whenever science has come to a crisis, a turning-point, where it ceased to go in its old direction, and where the way out could only be found by an examination of fundamental concepts, this was immediately felt to be a *philosophical* achievement. The solution of the antinomies of the infinite and Einstein's analysis of simultaneity are the most famous examples of this. If laying bare the structure of concepts, the analysis of language, the clarification of meaning is the peculiar task of the philosopher, then we must say that the philosophic attitude is an essential part of all scientific thought.[11]

This completes my necessarily brief survey of the nature of philosophy in general and I now relate the observations I have made to the study known as philosophy of education. From what has already been said one point should be clear, that philosophy of education is not to be regarded as a discipline in its own right, possessed of its own particular and distinctive techniques of enquiry. It is to be seen as an area of philosophical concern continuous with other areas of philosophical concern in that, broadly speaking, the same techniques, aimed at clarification and critical evaluation, operate. There is a discipline of philosophy and this discipline is used to illuminate, among other things, various types of discourse – mathematical, political, scientific, legal, educational, and so on. Hence any attempt to explicate the nature of philosophy of education necessarily involves explication of the nature of philosophy itself as a major component in that attempt. Philosophy of education is then to be distinguished from other 'philosophies of . . .' in that it is *about* educational discourse where the precise nature of 'about' is defined by reference to the preoccupations of philosophers in general: clarification of meaning, concern with types of justification, validity of arguments, and so on. Philosophy of education will be concerned with the clarification of concepts such as education, teaching, indoctrination, conditioning, training, socialisation, intelligence, needs, interests, creativity, understanding, motivation, authority, punishment, discipline, growth, and development. Additionally it will be concerned with the critical evaluation of arguments employing these concepts and others like them, arguments directly related to the practices and procedures of education.

It must be noted that in pursuit of these twin objectives educational philosophers will need to be familiar with the work of philosophers in other fields. Thus, one legitimate concern of the educational philosopher is the notion of moral education, and reflection on this notion demands reflection on the notion of morality, which is undeniably a concern of the moral philosopher. Again, among the concepts in the previous paragraph are intelligence, understanding and motivation, and these are studied by the philosopher of mind, as are the concepts of indoctrination, socialisation and authority by the political philosopher. These necessary excursions into other philosophical territories will occasion no methodological difficulties, for the techniques of enquiry in these territories will generally be the same as the techniques of enquiry in philosophy of education. All that differentiates the philosopher of mind, say, from the educational philosopher interested in concepts analysed by the philosopher of mind, is that the educational philosopher will be seeking to relate his overlapping enquiries to his primary interest – the practices and procedures of education.

Mention of moral and political philosophy as two branches of the subject with which the educational philosopher will need to be acquainted serves as a reminder of a point of some importance, the extent to which questions of value enter into the educational picture. Education, as we are often reminded, has to do with life or, at any rate, with the quality of life, and this means that considerations concerning what is to be valued, what is to be taken as worth while, necessarily arise. As Max Black puts it:

> All serious discussion of educational problems, no matter how specific, soon leads to a consideration of educational *aims*, and becomes a conversation about the good life, the nature of man, the varieties of experience.[12]

This raises a point of contention among contemporary philosophers. Is it any part of the educational philosopher's job to lay down the law as to what constitutes the good life? Making use of the distinction between first-order and second-order questions, surely dispute about the content of the good life is essentially first-order and hence not in the philosopher's province? The philosopher *as a man* has a perfect right to say in what he thinks the good life consists, but his philosophical expertise will not enable him to pronounce authoritatively on this issue. So runs the argument on one side. On the other side, some philosophers claim that it *is* specifically part of the philosophic enterprise to decide what constitutes the good life, that it *is* within the philosopher's province to legislate on this important matter. My own view is that the study of philosophy does not enable us to arrive at definitive conclusions concerning questions of value. At most, given *serious* discussion about such questions, the philosopher's strength lies in his ability to vet first-order discussion and debate for logical consistency, to lay bare assumption and presupposition, and to reveal spurious argumentation designed to preserve a position of vested interest.

In other words, he can help us to see and to understand clearly
the issues involved even if he is unable, in the last analysis, to
tell us exactly what we ought to do.

JUSTIFICATION OF THE STUDY OF PHILOSOPHY OF EDUCATION

I have already, in the previous section, made a number of
remarks which relate implicitly to the question of the justification of the study of philosophy of education, but I must now
tackle this question systematically and more comprehensively.
One point needs to be settled first of all. I am not here concerned
to evaluate the force of the argument that the study of philosophy of education is its own justification, that it is worth
undertaking for its own sake, that those who engage in it
because they find it intellectually challenging and because they
like doing it are under no compulsion to produce extraneous
reasons (having to do with usefulness, say) for so doing. I shall
simply bypass this aspect of justification and concentrate on
that aspect which has to do with why teachers ought to have
some knowledge of and some skill in philosophical analysis.

Consider, first of all, the fact that educational discussion and
debate is shot through with value judgments. In view of this
it is not in the least bit surprising to find such discussion and
debate marked by the emotive use of language, by the use of
'persuasive definitions', designed to bring about change in
people's value assessments. And designed to bring about change
in what people *do*, for very often there is a direct link between
what people value or do not value and what they do or do
not do. Put another way, we have here an instance in which
theory (educational debate) is directly related to practice (what
young people are made to do in educational institutions). Let us
take one or two specific examples. In Britain the term 'indoctrination' carries strong unfavourable emotive meaning, so
that to characterise a particular teaching transaction as 'indoc-
trinatory' might well result in the abandonment of that particular way of going about things. It therefore becomes a matter
of some importance to analyse the concept of indoctrination

with the object of seeing, as clearly as possible, its descriptive meaning. It will then, of course, only be legitimate to apply the corresponding term to instances which possess the features disclosed as a result of the analysis. Now, there is good reason to suppose that indoctrination is conceptually linked to the notion of doctrines, and that doctrines are to be distinguished from matters of fact. It follows, therefore, that if a teacher is transmitting matters of fact to his pupils he could not, logically, be in danger of indoctrinating them, whereas if a teacher is transmitting doctrine – political or religious doctrine, say – then he *is* in danger of doing so. Given that we are concerned to avoid indoctrination, we must be prepared to undertake the requisite analysis of the concept, to submit our arguments and conclusions to the scrutiny of others, and to join in the 'theoretical' discussion. The alternative seems to be for us to engage in educational activity with no awareness of what we are doing as far as indoctrination is concerned, so that we are incapable of rebutting fallacious reasoning, of which the following is a very good example.

> Every educational institution makes use of indoctrination. Children are indoctrinated with the multiplication table; they are indoctrinated with love of country; they are indoctrinated with the principles of chemistry and physics and mathematics and biology and nobody finds fault with indoctrination in these fields. Yet these are of small concern in the great business of life by contrast with ideas concerning God and man's relation to God, his duties to God, his neighbour and himself, man's nature and his supernatural destiny. The Catholic educator makes no apology for indoctrinating his students in these essential matters. To instruction in the arts and sciences, the Catholic university adds the notion of an unchanging standard of morality, the ideas of duty and responsibility to a personal and omnipotent God . . . [13]

As a second example, consider the notion of development. As used in educational contexts the term 'development' tends

C

to carry favourable emotive meaning; there is the suggestion that just so long as children are 'developing' all is well with the world. Along with this vague notion go equally vague notions of 'maturation', 'inner ripening' and 'readiness' ('He's not yet ready for reading'), and very often the total effect of subscribing to doctrines couched in terms of these notions consists in playing down the positive rôle of the teacher as one who, to some extent, directs learning, and elevating the importance of, say, children discovering things for themselves. Once more we see the possibility of a direct connection between ideas and action. And once more we see the danger of action being misguided in that it may be determined by what can only be called half-baked ideas. What is required, and what sustained philosophical critical thought can provide, is a way of seeing just what it means for a human being to develop. Are there different uses of the term? Is the concept of physical development essentially the same as the concept of mental development? Is there a difference between developing an argument and developing pneumonia and, if so, wherein lies the difference? Does it make sense to speak of someone 'developing along the wrong lines' and, if it does, how does this square with the image of the self-effacing teacher who simply leaves his charges to develop? Does he intercede if development is taking place along the wrong lines and, if so, how does he decide that 'wrong lines' are being followed? And so on. In posing questions like these we begin to uncover presuppositions and assumptions concerning people's beliefs, values and ideals, and this is something which must be done if we are to debate the worth of those underlying beliefs and ideals and the extent to which they ought to direct action. The whole burden of this questioning, critical approach stands in direct contrast to an approach, if 'approach' it can be called, dictated in advance by the impact of emotively-laden terminology together with its attendant slogans.

I have considered very briefly two examples of the way in which emotive meaning can, through its influence on people's attitudes, affect educational practice. Many other examples could have been taken – creativity, equality, discipline, freedom, integration in relation to curriculum subjects, and so on. Awareness of this emotive dimension of language, promoted by the study of philosophy, is certainly necessary if educational practice is not to be based upon a faulty 'theoretical' rationale. However, there is need for something more than simply this awareness. If a rational approach to the manifold problems of education is to be encouraged, then expertise in the overall critical evaluation of ideas is required, and this will involve the ability to detect fallacies in reasoning, the ability to distinguish statements of fact from statements of value and both from metaphysical statements. A very good example of the philosopher as critical thinker at work on an eminently practical issue is provided by Professor R. M. Hare in his book *Freedom and Reason*.[14] In the final chapter of the book, Hare considers the problem of racial conflict and provides a commentary on the logical status of the various types of argument which are encountered in debates on this problem. There are genuine factual questions (for example, are black people incapable of self-government?) of which Hare remarks that they:

> are not such as can be established or refuted by philosophical reasoning. They have to be shown to be true or false by the means appropriate to the examination of alleged facts of these kinds – i.e. by the objective study of history and, in appropriate cases, by social or psychological surveys and experiments.[15]

Then there are spurious factual arguments – for example, Germanic races have something in their hereditary make-up which gives them the right to oppress non-Germanic races. Two points are to be noted here. First, there is a metaphysical element involved: no tests are suggested for determining whether Germanic races *do* possess the 'something' which marks them off from non-Germanic races.[16] Second, given that Germanic races possess the 'something', how does this confer on them the right to persecute members of other races? Finally, there are disputes about values which can go on even when all the facts have been agreed – for example, someone may be simply horrified at the prospect of marriages between members of different races.

Suppose a 'hard-headed', 'realistic', 'down-to-earth' teacher says, 'I have no desire to spend my time philosophising in the ways you specify. I just want to be left to get on with the job of educating children.' There is surely only one reply to this kind of assertion: 'But what do you understand the job of educating children to consist in?' Amplifying this question we might ask, 'Do you see "educating the children" as teaching them the same sorts of things which you were taught when you were at school? Or is your object to get them to pass examinations? Perhaps you see your task as being to fit your pupils for jobs in the outside world? Or perhaps you are trying to produce people capable of critical thinking?' And so on. The point here is that the answers to our questions will reveal either that our hypothetical teacher *has* done some philosophical thinking about the concept of education, thus contradicting himself, or that he has done no thinking at all, in which case how on earth can he be left to get on with the job if he has no idea what it is? Similar sorts of consideration arise even if we take a more limited 'realistic' objection to the demand that philosophical thinking is necessary: 'I just want to be left to get on with the job of teaching my pupils history, Latin, mathematics, or what-have-you.' Pertinent questions to ask here would be, 'But what is the point of teaching them Latin or history?' 'Why not teach them how to play bingo rather than how to do equations?' 'What *kind* of history do you want to teach them?' It is of interest to note that in asking questions like these we are led inevitably into philosophical territory, for we find ourselves compelled to ask further questions, essentially philosophical ones, about the nature of knowledge and about the possibility of there being a limited number of 'ways of knowing' or a limited number of 'forms of knowledge'. Some very valuable work has been done in this area by Professor Hirst who has suggested that there are seven such forms – formal logic and mathematics, the physical sciences, understanding of our own and other people's minds, moral judgment, aesthetic experience, religion, and philosophy, 'each of which necessarily involves the use of concepts of a particular kind and a distinctive type of test for its objective claims'.[17] Clearly, if Hirst's analysis is correct, important consequences might well follow for curriculum planning and organisation at least as far as general education is concerned. Once more, then, we see ways in which the study of philosophy is directly relevant to educational practice in the sense that deciding on content of curricula is a practical issue.

In the final analysis, of course, it is still open to teachers to refuse to engage in any kind of thinking about the nature, point and purpose of their activities as teachers. They *could* simply refrain from considering any arguments of the type put forward above on the grounds that they do not wish to know about them. But, if this were their attitude, what sort of teachers would they then be? Presumably they would be no more than mere agents performing tasks specified by other people 'higher up' in an educational hierarchy, being told what to teach and how to teach. This rôle is certainly not one which is wished upon teachers in Britain at the present time. There is a great deal of talk these days about curriculum renewal, and in the opinion of many people teachers have a vital part to play in this, not only in the later stages of classroom implementation but also in the earlier discussion stages. Thus, consider the following statement taken from the Schools Council's *Working Paper No.* 2:

> The Council has also decided, as a matter of general policy, to make widely available its first thoughts on all major programmes of activity, so that these can be discussed by teachers and others concerned while the programmes are still at a fluid stage of development. If the Council's work is to be effective, it must be firmly rooted in classroom realities, and one way of achieving this is for the Council to invite the widest possible feedback of ideas, criticisms and suggestions for improvement in the early stages of major programmes of activity.[18]

Moreover, withdrawal by teachers from educational debate is unlikely to serve their own best interests, bearing in mind current moves to strengthen the position of teaching as a profession. Whatever the hall-marks of a profession are, one thing is clear: the very concept of a profession stands in marked contrast to the concept of a servile work force.

Exaggerated claims must not be made for the study of philosophy of education. It must not be supposed that solutions to the many and diverse educational problems with which we are faced are to be found simply by applying the techniques of philosophical analysis. We noted, when summarising Hare's 'commentary' on the racial problem, that as far as genuine factual questions are concerned the study of history and the results of sociological and psychological investigation are strictly relevant to obtaining answers. The same thing goes for many educational questions where matters of empirical fact are seen to be involved. Again, as was noted at the end of the first section of this paper, when it comes to deciding which of a number of competing value judgments ought to determine what is to be done in a particular situation, philosophy, in my opinion at any rate, cannot provide us with a means of selecting the 'right' judgment. This accounts for the peculiar intransigence of those educational problems which involve a profound value dimension, usually to do with the 'good life'. Such problems will be endlessly debated as long as man continues to survive. Certainly the following quotation from Aristotle (and, apart from stylistic peculiarities, it might have been taken from the writings of a contemporary educationist) gives us some reason for believing this:

> It is clear then that there should be laws laid down about education and that education itself must be made a national concern. But we must not forget the question what that education is to be, and how it is to be brought into operation. For in modern times there are opposing views about the practice of education. There is no general agreement about what the young should learn either in

relation to virtue or in relation to the best life; nor is it clear whether their education ought to be directed more towards the intellect than towards the character of the soul. The problem has been complicated by what we see happening before our eyes, and it is not certain whether training should be directed at things useful in life, or at those conducive to virtue, or at non-essentials. (All these answers have been given.) And there is no agreement as to what in fact does tend towards virtue. Men do not all prize most highly the same virtue, so naturally they differ also about the proper training for it.[19]

But while *exaggerated* claims must not be made for philosophy I hope that enough has been said to show the positive rôle that philosophical analysis has to play in thinking about educational issues and in arriving at decisions as to what is to be done in practice. There is indeed a value presupposition here in that philosophy is essentially a rational activity, and so in lauding philosophy I laud reason. Nevertheless, I would argue that, where an *intentional* activity like educating is concerned, the use of reason is indispensable in attempting to determine what to do and how to do it, and hence philosophy itself is indispensable.

HOW IS PHILOSOPHY OF EDUCATION TO BE TAUGHT?

If philosophy of education is essentially an analytic, critical activity, as I have argued, then certain consequences would seem to follow concerning the ways in which it should be taught. The lecture would not seem to be a satisfactory teaching medium on the grounds that lecturing is more suited to the transmission of information, to surveying, say, research in a somewhat narrow field when the results of that research are unpublished or are to be found only in obscure journals. The lecture is *not* the way to make people adept at critical thinking, *not* the way to enable them to master philosophic, analytic *skills*. As with skills generally, probably the best way to get

people to command the philosophic skills is to insist on their
being practised, and this will involve writing and talking
philosophy, having our arguments and conclusions subjected
to the criticism of our peers and tutors, having to defend our
arguments, and so on. And activities of this kind are best
carried on in the one-to-one tutorial, or in the seminar consisting of about a dozen participants. The one-to-one tutorial
has distinct advantages. It gives the teacher the opportunity
to ascertain the student's level of attainment in philosophy and
to go on from there, to tailor instruction to the student's
capabilities, to encourage him to put forward his own ideas
knowing that they will be taken seriously, and to get over the
fundamental idea that on a number of issues the student has to
work towards his *own* position and that the teaching of philosophy does not consist in the teacher putting forward truths
to be learned and reproduced in examinations. The seminar
also possesses some of these advantages, or can possess them if
the seminar leader does not use the occasion to deliver a mini-
lecture. But there are disadvantages, well-known ones such as
hopelessly unstructured discussion, the problem of the silent
member or of the dominating, loquacious member, failure to
prepare for the topic except on the part of the person who is
introducing it, and so on. Some of these disadvantages can be
overcome (careful planning of topics for discussion, duplica-
tion in advance of the paper to be read or ensuring that every-
one has a copy of a volume of collected papers, say, that is to
be used as a source for topics), and even if not all of them can
be overcome, nevertheless the seminar, properly conducted,
brings home the importance in philosophy of the interchange
of ideas directed towards the solution of common problems.

An obvious objection to this description (and to the implicit
prescription) of a somewhat ideal state of affairs must now be
considered. The time available for or devoted to philosophy
in the three-year course in a number of colleges of education
is strictly limited; in addition there is usually a shortage of
members of staff capable of conducting a philosophy seminar.
What usually happens is that the 'resident' philosopher gives a

number of lectures, usually late in the course, to an audience of some 250 students (sometimes more, sometimes less), and these lectures are followed by discussion in groups a number of which are 'led' by people with no particular expertise, and perhaps no particular interest, in philosophy. This is manifestly unsatisfactory. A number of suggestions designed to ameliorate the situation could be made – more time devoted to the subject enabling the philosopher to conduct seminars, persuading members of staff with more than a marginal interest in philosophy to attend courses – but if these suggestions are unacceptable all that seems possible is to attempt to make what one can of the block lecture system. Here an observation made by John Wisdom may prove fruitful:

> In a sense, philosophy cannot be taught – any more than one can teach riding or dancing or musical appreciation. However, philosophers can be made. They can be made in two ways, namely by practice and by precept. The first method is the one usually adopted by lecturers in philosophy or performing philosophers. They themselves perform philosophic antics in front of their students, interlarded with anecdotes about the antics of contemporary performers. This is called giving a course in modern philosophy. Or, they tell stories about performers of the past: then they are giving a course in the history of philosophy. Sometimes their students are able to imitate these performances; they are the 'good students'.[20]

If a lecture *has* to be given to a large audience, then the philosopher must contrive to avoid the inherent danger in all lecturing – the authority delivering 'the goods' – and concentrate on getting over the technique of philosophising (the 'philosophic antics'). Something of benefit may well result for, although I said earlier on that probably the best way of getting people to command skills is to insist that they practise them, another way consists in demonstrating the skills so that the learner can imitate. Ideally, of course, a skilled performer is wanted to comment on the imitation but this may not be possible. The 'performer' may decide to conduct his 'antics' alone – a sort of one-man Socratic dialogue. But it may be preferable to think in terms of two people 'performing'. Certainly two philosophers, or a philosopher and a psychologist, discussing a problem on which they hold contrasting views is far more likely than the set lecture to help students to see that there are no cut and dried answers to, say, fundamental value questions and that ultimately they, the students, must think things through for themselves.

One final point must be made concerning not so much the form the teaching of philosophy should take as the way in which the subject is introduced. (Once more my comments are related to students as a whole, and not just to those who are specialising in philosophy of education.) It seems to me that if students are to see philosophy as applicable to their classroom concerns, then the study of the subject must arise out of those concerns. Thus, the way into the study of moral philosophy ought not to consist in a series of lectures on Moore's intuitionism or Hare's prescriptivism, but ought to begin with the questioning of a group of teachers along such lines as these: 'Do you see it as part of your job to be morally educating your pupils?' 'When you read that story to those eight-year-olds the other day, did you choose it because it made a moral point?', and so on. We will get to Moore's intuitionism and Hare's prescriptivism this way even though we may decide not to use precisely these names. Again, a number of philosophical issues arise in connection with curriculum studies. Within the time devoted to curricular subjects, questions relating to objectives of teaching and to aims of education could quite easily and legitimately be raised. Subsequent more formal treatment of the philosophical issues – in block lectures if necessary – will then no longer come out of the blue and occasion derisory comments of the type, 'What has all this got to do with teaching?' Of course, we have the manpower problem still. One philosopher cannot do things of the kind I have indicated with all students. What, ideally, is wanted is concern on the part of all lecturers and tutors for philosophical matters and a realisation of their fundamental importance. In recent years we have come some way towards this, but there is still a long way to go.

References

1 Russell, B., *A History of Western Philosophy*. Allen and Unwin, 1946, pp. 10-11.
2 Peters related this anecdote at a Conference on the Education and Training of Teachers at Avery Hill College, 2-6 January 1967. Cf. also Warnock, G. J., in *The Revolution in Philosophy*. Macmillan, 1956, p. 125: 'I believe that it could not easily be denied that in philosophy an unusually high proportion of what has been written, and indeed is written, could not unjustly be described as nonsense, and it is no service to anyone to pretend otherwise.'
3 Ayer, A. J., *Language, Truth and Logic*. Gollancz, 2nd edition, 1946, p. 31.
4 King, A. R., Jr., and Brownell, J. A., *The Curriculum and the Disciplines of Knowledge*. New York, John Wiley, 1966, p. 2.
5 Cf. Ryle, G., in *The Revolution in Philosophy*, p. 8: 'The story of twentieth-century philosophy is very largely the story of this notion of sense or meaning.'
6 This example is borrowed from Scheffler, I., *The Language of Education*. Springfield, Ill., Charles C. Thomas, 1960, p. 19.
7 Stevenson, C. L., *Ethics and Language*. New Haven, Conn., Yale University Press, 1944, p. 210.
8 Wittgenstein, L., *Philosophical Investigations*. Oxford, Blackwell, 2nd edition, 1958, p. 31.
9 Geach, P. T., *Mental Acts*. Routledge and Kegan Paul, 1957, p. 13.
10 Wisdom, J., *Problems of Mind and Matter*. Cambridge University Press (paperback edition), 1963, p. 2.
11 Waismann, F., *The Principles of Linguistic Philosophy*. Macmillan ('Papermacs'), 1968, p. 14. See also the Symposium entitled *Quanta and Reality*, Hutchinson, 1962, especially the discussion between Professors Pryce and Bohm, pp. 61-83.
12 Black, M., 'A note on "philosophy of education" ', in Lucas, C. J., *What is Philosophy of Education?* Macmillan, 1969, p. 284.
13 From McGucken's *The Catholic Way in Education*, quoted in Brubacher, J. S. (ed.), *Eclectic Philosophy of Education*. Englewood Cliffs, N.J., Prentice-Hall, 2nd edition, 1962, pp. 335-6.
14 Hare, R. M., *Freedom and Reason*. Oxford University Press (paperback) 1965.
15 *Ibid.*, p. 206.

16 Note that I use the term 'metaphysical' in a relatively restricted sense.
    A statement is metaphysical if no observations can be made relevant to
    establishing the truth/falsity of the statement. See O'Connor, D. J.,
    An Introduction to the Philosophy of Education. Routledge and Kegan
    Paul, 1957, p. 17, Note i; pp. 44-5.
17 Hirst, P. H., and Peters, R. S., *The Logic of Education.* Routledge and
    Kegan Paul, 1970, p. 63. See also Hirst, P. H., 'Liberal education and the
    nature of knowledge', in Archambault, R. D. (ed.), *Philosophical
    Analysis and Education.* Routledge and Kegan Paul, 1967.
18 The Schools Council, *Working Paper No. 2, Raising the school leaving
    age.* H.M.S.O., 1965, p. iii.
19 Aristotle, *The Politics,* VIII, 2. [The translation is T. A. Sinclair's in
    the Penguin Classics, 1962, p. 300.]
20 Wisdom, J., *op. cit.,* p. 2. The precept method need not detain us. Of
    it Wisdom says that it 'has not been much used' because even good
    philosophers, like many good riders, have been 'unable to say what it is
    about their methods which makes them good'.

History of Education

Malcolm Seaborne

WHAT IS HISTORY OF EDUCATION?

The first question we need to ask ourselves is: 'What exactly is comprised under the heading of the history of education?' The term itself has been in use since the last century, when education as a subject was included in courses for intending teachers at colleges and universities. Closely linked with the history of education as originally taught was the history of educational ideas, which explained the 'philosophies' of certain so-called 'great educators' of the past, such as Aristotle and Plato, Locke and Rousseau, Herbart and (more recently) Dewey.

When the history of education first found its way into British college courses it reflected, perhaps inevitably, the contemporary state of historical studies generally by concentrating on the political and constitutional aspects of development, just as the emphasis in many history departments at the universities of the time was on constitutional growth, culminating in the triumph of parliamentary democracy in Britain. The history of education was, however, particularly prone to a legalistic approach because British teacher-training colleges of the nineteenth century, though founded by voluntary bodies, depended on financial grants from the State, as of course did the schools in which the students taught on qualifying. State control through the official 'Codes', and the increasing part played by national legislation following the passing of the 1870 Elementary Education Act, were further reasons for considering

the growth of educational administration as the essential core
of the history of education as then conceived. Linked with
this, too, was the idea of progress through the increasing inter-
vention of the central government and, following the passing
of the 1902 Education Act, of the local education authorities. In
this way, the history of education was used to show that education had gradually improved – a linear development concerned
more with the increasingly complex apparatus of public control
than with any consideration of the quality of education as such.

In so far as 'quality' was considered, it was by adopting a
similar idea of progression towards modern enlightenment,
derived from the study of the 'great educators'. Their ideas
were studied in order to provide a composite model to guide
the modern teacher, and the *raison d'être* of these studies was
that through them the accumulated wisdom of past education
might be acquired. The approach was therefore essentially
eclectic – an idea of Aristotle here, or Rousseau there, leading
up to a modern ideal which claimed to incorporate all that was
best in the educational thought of the past.

These approaches may still be found today, but are rapidly
being displaced. So far as the history of educational ideas is
concerned, most present-day philosophers of education reject
any claim to dispense absolute truths and as a result they are
far less interested in those philosophers of the past who themselves formulated prescriptive rules for the educationist. It has
in any case come to be realised that the 'educational' parts of
the writings of past thinkers cannot be abstracted without a
thorough study being made of the entire philosophical systems
of the thinkers being investigated. Historians, too, are sceptical
of the old approach. Most of them would prefer to see the
ideas of past writers considered in relation to the social conditions which influenced them – to study Plato, for example, in
the context of the city state and the actual education provided
in ancient Greece – and also to consider what effect, if any,
these various ideas had on subsequent educational practice.

The historical aspect of education is also now conceived of
in much broader terms than formerly. Legislation and admini-

stration are now regarded as worthy of study not so much in
their own right but as a reflection of changes in society as a
whole. Thus it is not enough to know what alterations in the
law were made by, say, the Education Act of 1902 or that of
1944: we need to know why these Acts were passed when
they were, in response to what social pressures, and with what
effects on the structure not only of the educational system but
of society generally.

The former concentration on purely administrative changes
also left out many aspects of educational history now regarded
as of vital importance. In particular, the actual content of
education is now seen to be of great interest, since changes in
curriculum not only reflect social changes in a unique way but
also provide an opportunity to assess the impact made by
education on its actual 'consumers'. Indeed, many historians
now consider that we have for far too long looked at education
from above, as it were – from the point of view of politicians,
administrators and others outside the system – rather than
from the point of view of the children, young people and
adults being taught in classrooms and lecture-halls. With this
change of viewpoint is coming an increasing interest in what is
sometimes called the 'archaeology' of education, that is, those
physical remains long thought unworthy of notice, such as
children's text-books and exercises, equipment and furniture,
and school buildings.

A shift of interest is also exemplified by the new attitude
towards the history of individual educational institutions. The
number of school, college and university histories is very large,
but their limitations are now becoming more fully apparent.
It is of course true that to concentrate on an individual school
gives a certain coherence to an account of its historical development and may well be of interest to its former pupils. But by
far the greater number of school histories have been written
without taking account of general developments in education,
or even of the history of the locality in which the school is
situated. The result is that, at best, the majority of school
histories provide only the raw material for meaningful work

in the history of education, for it is only when we begin to
compare one school with another, or to look at local developments in education in the context of the more general history
of a large town, or the wider area of a county or economic
region, that significant points begin to emerge.

A further broadening of the concept of what is comprised
in the history of education has resulted from a redefinition of
the meaning of education itself. Until quite recently, it has
been conceived of as concerned almost exclusively with the
educational institutions in which formal teaching takes place.
The work of social historians and sociologists has, however,
made clear the importance of, for example, the home and the
social milieu in which a child is brought up, and – in the case
of adult education – of the social and economic position of its
recipients. The historians of cultural and literary change have
also shown how attitudes have often altered quite independently
of the system of formal education. This in turn has led to
consideration of what is now called 'informal' education as
worthy of detailed historical study. Thus there is a relatively
new appreciation of the fact that only a small minority of
children before about 1800 were educated at school at all,
though the rest were still being educated in some form or
other. For example, the influence of printed books in the
sixteenth and seventeenth centuries and of the 'chap-books 'of
the eighteenth century has recently been stressed, and it is also
clear that, even after the introduction of compulsory universal
education towards the end of the nineteenth century, many
attitudes were formed and skills learnt by agencies other than
those provided by schools, colleges and universities.

Indeed, we may say that an increasing number of historians
of education see their subject as essentially a branch of general
social and intellectual history, and one in which 'formal'
education often plays only a subsidiary part. It is also increasingly being realised that educational institutions are themselves
reflections of the changing social structure and can only be
understood by reference to such phenomena as fluctuations in
population, changes in religious attitudes, alterations in the

structure of the family and in the relationships between the social classes, which are themselves in a constant state of flux.

It is clear at this point that historians of education, like those working in many other branches of history, have been influenced by the rapid growth of the social sciences in the present century and particularly since the Second World War. Perhaps we may draw a comparison here with the influence on historical study of developments in the natural sciences towards the end of the nineteenth century, an influence which has often been remarked upon. For then it was that new 'scientific' approaches were adopted, especially with regard to the authentication of historical facts. Such a development was necessary if the mass of legend, inaccurate transcriptions and unauthenticated texts was to be transformed into reliable raw material for the historian to work upon. Some scholars went further and tried to show that it might be possible for the historian, by accumulating all the surviving data of the past, to formulate general historical laws which, like the laws of science, could be tested against new data and even used for predictive purposes. These hopes, as is well known, never materialised, because the 'facts' proved to be both overwhelming in number and yet incomplete on many vital points. It is now generally agreed that every historian must make a selection of the raw material available to him and that historical interpretation is essentially a personal matter, so that though it is to be hoped that an individual historian's interpretation may win general acceptance, it cannot be expected that his work will lead to the formulation of general laws. Many historians would therefore subscribe to the view that in organising their material they cannot do more than provide a colligation or grouping of the material in a significant way – intelligible, that is to say, to their contemporary readers – which may suggest provisional answers to historical problems but not supply final solutions.[1]

It is probable that, just as the advances in the natural sciences proved very useful but not ultimately convincing for the study of history at the end of the nineteenth century, so the more

D

recent advances in the social sciences are having a similarly important but not overwhelming influence. Let us look at the positive side first, and particularly the effect of the social sciences on the study of the history of education. A recent writer on this subject takes as the theme of her exposition the definition of education given by the sociologist Durkheim.[2] She quotes with approval his very broad description of education as:

> the influence exercised by adult generations on those that are not yet ready for social life. Its object is to arouse and to develop in the child a certain number of physical, intellectual and moral states which are demanded of him by both the political society as a whole and the special milieu for which he is specifically destined.

Though this is couched in very general terms, it is in some respects more limiting than the views held by some present-day historians of education. In particular, it appears to confine the study to children only, and it also seems to suggest that children as such do not experience 'social life'. If social life is by definition that lived only by adults, then perhaps we are entitled to ask whether some part of a child's education might not be devoted to studies appropriate to his childish state, quite apart from any possible relevance to later adulthood. The use of the words 'demanded' and 'destined' also suggests an all-pervading and rigid form of adult control which many educationists would find repellent.

It is nevertheless clear that modern sociological studies have had considerable influence on the work of historians, many of whom have taken account both of sociological theory and methodology. The former often aims at establishing models for social development and the latter typically stresses the importance of quantified data. While it may be freely admitted that the development of the social sciences has led historians to ask new questions and to seek for greater precision in formulating their answers, many historians would argue that the construction of models and of universal (or even 'middle-range') theories is not always possible or desirable and that not all historical phenomena are amenable to quantification. Basically it has to be recognised that the assumptions made by the historian are different from those of the social scientist, for the historian takes his stand on the contingency of human behaviour.[3]

The writer referred to above, after quoting Durkheim, goes on to suggest that historians of education should be able to establish 'the independent status and nature of historical enquiry' – independent, that is to say, of the study of education as such. This raises the question of the relationship of the study of the history of education to the other disciplines of education. Many educational historians at the present time would probably subscribe to the view expressed earlier in this book that education is a field of study and not itself a discipline. The task of the historian, therefore, is to show what light his particular discipline can throw on education as an activity. On this view, he must regard the history of education as a branch of history and find in the discipline of history both the methodology and ultimate justification of what he does.

Some historians of education would go beyond this. While admitting their debt to general history and to the techniques developed by historians, they would make a value-judgment about their subject. Because they regard the educational process as of supreme importance, they would claim that it deserves more intensive study than some other branches of history; and also that it must be studied in unison with the other main disciplines of education. Thus a member of an education department in a college of education has recently claimed that 'history of education is qualitatively different from many other categories of history'[4] and a professor of education similarly states that 'when history is rewritten education should take its proper place not merely as an adjunct to the historical process but as one of the chief factors conditioning men's outlook and aspirations'.[5]

It must be admitted that at the present stage of development, the question of the relationship of the history of education to the discipline of history and of the various disciplines to the study of education has not been fully settled. At present we are seeing the emergence of the various disciplines which bear on education from the welter of topics taught in colleges and departments of education, and further thought will have to be given to how they can best cohere together.

JUSTIFICATION OF THE STUDY OF HISTORY OF EDUCATION

Let us now consider in more detail what may properly be regarded as the value and general relevance of the study of the history of education. What little evidence is available suggests that the history of education, as at present understood and taught in colleges of education, is not regarded as of much importance. This was the conclusion reached in a survey made in 1967 and later published in the journal *Education for Teaching*.[6] This survey was concerned with the content of the courses on what were called the 'principles of education', and the results were analysed in terms of 100 separate topics which appeared in college syllabuses in various parts of the country. The 'importance' of the various topics for intending teachers was then assessed by groups of practising teachers, college staff, students, L.E.A. staff and members of education committees. The results were quantified and the 100 topics placed in order of importance. Six of the topics which were rated in the 'top ten' concerned teaching methods, and two concerned the curriculum. The topic on 'The 1944 Education Act and its subsequent modification' rated 70th out of the 100, that on 'The development of educational provision from about 1800 to 1944' as 94th, while that on 'Educational provision in Britain before about 1800' was bottom of the list. The other disciplines of education – psychology, sociology and 'fundamental problems' (which appeared as the nearest category to what is now more generally known as the philosophy of education) – fared only marginally better.

At first glance this survey might appear to lend support to those who assert that colleges of education should concentrate on teaching methods and ignore 'theoretical' studies remote from immediate classroom problems. The list of 100 topics is of interest, however, more as a reflection of the unstructured state of educational studies in the colleges of the 1960s than of anything else – the list is like a geological record accumulated from a long period of disparate studies in the colleges. In particular, the topics grouped under the 'history of education' relate almost entirely to narrow administrative history of the kind which historians are increasingly condemning.

The basic assumption behind the survey – that subjects can be arranged hierarchically in a purely vocational context – can also be questioned. Certainly the 'importance' or 'relevance' of the history of education has in the past been thought of much too narrowly by trying to relate it immediately to the task of the classroom teacher. Such concern has perhaps been inevitable, since colleges of education have recruited only students intending to teach, just as educational studies for most graduates have been telescoped into a single year of post-graduate study, about a third of which is taken up with teaching practice. It can, in fact, be claimed that 'many of the methods and data that the historian of education uses, many of the attitudes and approaches he adopts as he studies the past . . . are relevant to the task that the teacher faces in becoming a better practitioner'.[7] It is also true that the teacher today does not spend all his time in front of a class of children: he has to work increasingly with other adults – his colleagues, his pupils' parents, and the public at large – so that more is required of him than pedagogical expertise. These are, however, relatively long-term considerations which justify the rigorous study of the broader aspects of education. The majority of students, as our system of teacher-training is at present constituted, are concerned first and foremost (and quite naturally) to become proficient classroom practitioners, and much of their initial training must therefore consist of on-the-job experience, with major emphasis on the subject-matter of the lessons and the techniques of class control, and minimal attention to wider educational issues, however important they may be in the long run and however vital, again in the longer

term, they may be for sound practical teaching over a full
working life.

Fortunately we can consider this question of importance or
'value' in a wider context than that provided by initial courses
for intending teachers. History is a well-established subject in
schools and universities and there is an extensive literature of
historiography.[8] It must in honesty be admitted, however,
that history as a whole (and not merely the history of education) has not always been well taught, and that doubts have
been raised as to its value and 'relevance' in a world reaching
out into space and more than ever concerned with the problems of the present and future. The study of history has often
been said to have largely replaced that of the classics as a fundamental training in the humanities, but there are some indica-
tions that, just as the classics have been increasingly ignored
because of their apparent 'irrelevance', so history in some of its
forms has more recently been coming under attack. In the
satirical 'short educational dictionary' compiled by Kingsley
Amis and Robert Conquest, history is defined as an 'obso-
lescent, irrelevant study . . . an agglomeration of irrelevant
"facts" and bourgeois propaganda'.[9] Such a view may conceiv-
ably be held by some radical students, but the charge of
irrelevance has been heard more widely and needs further
consideration.

There are those who would dismiss the charge of irrelevance
out of hand and argue that any subject which is intellectually
demanding, or simply interesting, can be justified on those
grounds alone. Others might agree with Professor Elton, who
thinks that one of the chief values for young people studying
history is that it counteracts the 'extraordinary naïvety' shown
by students who 'proclaim their immaturity by their exceptional concern with themselves alone'. Elton also gives one of
the traditional defences of historical study when he says that
'at a proper academic level, history provides an exceptional
training in analytical thought, tempered by reasoned reflection
and an understanding of the possible, which makes it superior
as a school for the man of business and affairs to either the

natural or the social sciences'.[10] Another leading academic
historian points out that 'business and government of all kinds
require, in addition to specialist knowledge, a general capacity
to deal with complex human situations' of the kind with which
the study of history makes us familiar; and he adds that 'it is
not so surprising . . . that the highest-paid graduates in industry
by their middle thirties are historians. Who else can get, outside industry itself, the necessary breadth of vision and general
training?'[11]

All this may be true, so far as it goes. But does it go far
enough? The prospect of high earnings in industry or administration does not always attract the serious-minded student, or
satisfy the idealistic longings of youth. Indeed, it may seem
odd that a defence of history on the highest intellectual plane
should conclude with an argument based on wholly material
advantage. In any event, the question of relevance cannot be
disposed of so readily, and has risen in an acute form in connection with the detailed work of syllabus-construction at all
levels of the educational system. Since this is inevitably a
continuing process, and since the place of the history of education in the general field of historical study has not yet been
fully determined, it is necessary to examine this question in
more detail.

The traditional view that history is worth teaching because
of the general intellectual qualities it fosters (analytical power,
verbal expression, and so on) can presumably be applied to
any period or aspect of history – for example, to early Byzan-
tine as much as to, say, modern British history; in this view,
the content is relatively unimportant so long as its study pro-
duces the desired qualities. Such a view has, however, come up
against two difficulties. In the first place, many students and
their teachers are concerned to relate their studies to the pressing
problems of the contemporary world; they are more than ever
aware of the material and spiritual suffering of mankind and
hope that by studying these problems historically they will
obtain a better understanding of them and perhaps contribute
to their solution. Such considerations lie behind the increasing

demand in the schools and universities for the study of 'contemporary history', and also behind the desire to study history in a world context rather than on the traditional national basis.

In the second place, some confusion is apparent from the multiplication of historical studies. As the study of history has developed during the present century, so new branches have been established: beginning with constitutional and political history, there grew up, largely as a result of inter-war pressures, a concern with economic and diplomatic history; similarly, as other countries have become more aware of their own history, and as the nations of the world have reacted increasingly upon each other, so other aspects have had to be taken into account. Thus a recent *Introduction for the Intending Student* (1970) includes chapters not only on ancient, mediaeval and early modern history, but also on modern British political history, social and economic history, local and regional history, and on the histories of modern Europe, the United States, Latin America, Africa, Asia, and the history of science.[12] A similarly very wide range is included in the recent book *New Movements in the Study and Teaching of History* (1970), both as regards subject-matter and methods of study, and there are inevitable contradictions in the views put forward by the various contributors.[13]

In view of this proliferation, we are bound to ask what case there can possibly be for adding further to the list by promoting the history of education as an independent or at least semi-independent branch of historical study. Here it seems to me that one has frankly to recognise that in a changing world and in a situation where knowledge is expanding rapidly, history has become a polymathic study. It could still be true, however, that, varied as the content has become, the essential intellectual qualities which history develops remain fundamentally the same. For, whatever branch of history may be studied, there must be the same respect for the rules of historical evidence; there is still the imaginative and intellectual effort needed in attempting to enter into the minds and hearts of people in other ages and civilisations; and there is still the essential human sympathy needed to try to understand the past in all its complexity. The study of almost any branch of history can also perform the vital service of providing a frame of reference to the present. The realisation that changes have taken place in the past, that our present situation is not a permanent one and might be changed by human effort as sometimes in the past, can be a liberating influence. The historian is constantly probing the past to find answers to the questions he puts to it and it may also be legitimate (though not all historians would agree) to use historical evidence to test working hypotheses or at least to cast light on the direction of our present policies.

The interaction of the past, present and future is far too complex to permit of detailed analysis. It is helpful, however, to bear in mind the distinction first made by Professor Oakeshott between the 'historical past' and the 'practical past'.[14] A study of the 'practical past' means that we in the present look at the events of the past only from the point of view of their practical effects upon us, here and now. As W. H. Burston has remarked, teachers who concentrate on this view of the past are not really teaching history at all: 'it is not history which they teach, for they *never get out of the present*' (my italics).[15] There can be no doubt that it is the effort required to understand people and events in the past which constitutes one of the most valuable parts of historical study: it is this which stimulates historical imagination, breaks down prejudice and increases our knowledge of human nature. At the same time, it is clear that the content of what is studied at any given time is dependent on our present interests. Every historian is concerned to interpret the past in terms which are intelligible to his own contemporaries, and any survey of historical writing will show very clearly how contemporary attitudes influenced not only the content of what was studied but also the method of presentation.[16] We in the second half of the twentieth century are therefore bound to reflect the concerns of our own time. In so far as historians have, for example, social consciences, or deep interest in particular aspects of our present situation, they are bound to want to relate current problems to their historical findings and to contribute to the various debates now in progress. (To try, as some historians seem to do, to 'live in the past' must surely be regarded as a form of escapism.) Fortunately, historians who do not hesitate to enter the past in order to return better-informed into the present have, or should have, the traditional safeguards demanded by the use of historical evidence and the need for careful analysis and clear exposition in non-technical language.

The justification for the study of any branch of history can therefore be considered at various levels. We can, for example, stress the general intellectual qualities fostered and cultural interests aroused – virtues which could be cited to justify studies however remote in time or specialised in content (for example, the study of ancient Sparta, or seventeenth-century France). The argument would then presumably be that, apart from the minority remaining to teach the subject themselves, the majority would go on to apply the more general abilities learnt to some other more directly 'practical' job, or perhaps to pursue the interests aroused on a leisure-time basis. Let us suppose, however, that we are firmly convinced that certain present-day activities are more worth pursuing than others, whether it be in the realm of religion, music, literature or some kind of social work. In such a case, we would surely be justified in concentrating our attention on the historical manifestations of that particular aspect, with the more general intellectual qualities fostered by the subject regarded as a kind of bonus rather than as the *raison d'être* of the study itself. If, further, we acknowledge that a large proportion of the population is bound to be subjected to education in some form or another, then we are also surely justified in arguing that every discipline which can fruitfully be applied to the study of education, including the historical, should be fully explored. The study of the history of education may therefore be regarded as having a distinct *social* purpose, quite apart from the personal satisfactions to be derived from its study, or the more general intellectual qualities developed.

It is worth noting in this context that some historians working in other fields are also feeling the need to find a social purpose for their work. The idea of progress explored earlier in this century by J. B. Bury, for example, has not stood the test of time, and certainly the view of history as a linear progression, such as bedevilled the study of the history of education in the early training colleges, has been exploded. But the idea has recently been revived in more realistic form by J. H. Plumb, as the way out of what he calls 'the historian's dilemma' – that is, the proliferation of historical studies, the increasing specialisation leading to research in ever more marginal fields, and the general lack of certainty which many historians feel about the ultimate value of their work.[17] He writes:

> By progress in history, I mean nothing more than that man's increasing control over his environment is historically verifiable, as are its consequential results, namely, that this increasing control has rendered more and more of men's lives longer, healthier, more secure, and more leisured, and that the species itself has become more numerous, more firmly established, more in control of the physical world.

Plumb goes on to speak of the material and intellectual progress evident in the last 7000 years and considers that:

> It ought to be the historian's duty to lay bare these processes by which social progress has taken place, in the hope that knowledge and understanding may lead to their acceleration and development. So, too, should they concern themselves with those factors in society which have inhibited growth and change and, even at times, led to retrogression, so that these might, in the future, be avoided.

It must immediately be admitted, however, that the study of the history of education has a long way to go before it becomes established as a fully-grown branch, contributing to our understanding both of general historical developments and of the educational process. The historical aspect of education

has in general been taught in so attenuated a form as to be
treated by many students with the lack of comprehension, if
not the open contempt, which in this form it largely deserves.
It is also true that too few historians have applied their skills
to the elucidation of educational problems, and, although there
are certainly some notable exceptions, the study of the history
of education is still, as a leading historian has recently remarked,
at 'a primitive stage . . . both in the collection of data and the
formulation of concepts'.[18] Perhaps this is too harsh a judgment, since much has been written on the history of education
and some of it is certainly of lasting value.[19] It is nevertheless
easier to see where the subject is deficient than to point to
advances already made. Much of the essential source material
is still unexplored, and as a result there is a notable lack of
well-documented monographs on the subject. This in turn has
meant that the general text-books on the history of education
have tended to concentrate on administrative changes, or on
what have rightly been called the 'surface phenomena' of
educational history. Nor has the history of education yet
benefited to any degree by considering it in relation to allied
fields, apart perhaps from some aspects of sociology. Local
educational studies have only rarely applied the more fruitful
approaches to local history developed since the Second World
War; demographic studies likewise are only just beginning to
impinge on the history of education through the study of
levels of literacy; and architectural history has only recently
been related to the development of school buildings. The study
of European and world history which has developed rapidly
in universities and schools has hardly begun to influence the
history of education. Certainly, 'comparative education' has
been taught in some places, but until very recently there has
been an almost total lack of historical perspective, so that
either the information supplied soon becomes out of date or the
reader is given a detailed description of educational systems in
other countries with insufficient explanation of how they came
to be as they are.

There are, however, clear signs that many of these deficiencies are being made good. The formation of a History of Education Society in 1967 has encouraged new developments in colleges and departments of education, and more historians are taking account of educational changes. Given further expansion of the subject, there can be no doubt that its value in increasing our understanding of the educational process will become more widely recognised. If, as seems likely, some colleges of education develop into liberal arts colleges or at least recruit on a broader basis than hitherto, there is the possibility that education, including the history of education, will be studied in a wider context and with much greater profit than in the past. When this happens, it will be found not only that student-teachers have a more thorough theoretical knowledge than at present but that their development as classroom practitioners will also have improved.

HOW IS HISTORY OF EDUCATION TO BE TAUGHT?

Let us turn in this final section to the question of how the history of education may best be taught. At present it is taught almost exclusively in colleges and university departments of education. Much time in the three-year college course is taken up with the study of the subjects to be taught to children of various age-groups, and much to teaching practice in local schools. At the universities, the fact that undergraduates enter professions of many kinds helps to ensure that their degree courses are usually broadly-based and can arouse – at least in some students – wide intellectual interests. Most of those who decide to teach after taking their degree have a further year's course, which attempts to introduce students to the long-term benefits of educational studies and the short-term requirements of actually teaching children, a combination which, as we have seen, is not easily achieved in the time available. The coming of the Bachelor of Education degree, however, which involves a fourth year at a college of education for some of those who have already been recognised as qualified teachers, and the diploma and higher degree work which exists (if mainly on a part-time basis) for practising teachers, gives more opportunity for the detailed study of the disciplines of education.

How can we ensure that the time available (even if, as at present, frequently inadequate) can best be used? So far as the history of education is concerned, it is clearly sensible to take account of developments in the historical field generally, since teaching methods have received considerable attention in recent years (for example, in the journal *Teaching History*, published by the Historical Association at regular intervals since May 1969). On the other hand, it has sometimes been alleged that history, more than most other subjects, has responded very slowly, at least at school level, to the 'curriculum development' movement which has in the last few years led to many new publications on teaching, particularly of science and mathematics. It may perhaps be said that history teachers, like most teachers on the 'arts side', are as much concerned with the 'affective' as the 'cognitive' side of learning – that is, with the development of attitudes and emotions as distinct from intellectual skills, if indeed it is genuinely possible to make this now popular distinction. They are not necessarily opposed to 'objective-type' questions (those which require answers which are clearly right or wrong), but they realise the limitations of such an approach to the testing of historical knowledge. They also realise that essay-type answers, though difficult to mark and incorporating a considerable subjective element, are nevertheless essential if any real assessment is to be made of the skills of communication needed by the student of history. Some, too, may sense that the greater the apparent objectivity of the test applied, the more devastating is likely to be the effect on the child who scores low marks.

Some of the new techniques being developed may not therefore be equally suitable for all subjects in the curriculum. On the other hand, the C.S.E. examination, with its opportunity for more experimental work, has been taken up as much by history teachers as by teachers of other subjects. Some bad habits have persisted (especially the excessive taking of notes), but are by no means confined to the teaching of history. There is, however, one basic procedure which has remained entrenched and to which history teachers are perhaps particularly prone. This is to look upon the syllabus as a corpus of knowledge which has to be put over to the children at all costs. This may arise from the chronological nature of history, which tends to lead secondary-school teachers on step by step and to make them feel uneasy if one or more steps are left out. It has been pointed out that children's sense of historical time appears to develop relatively late, but some teachers argue that it is only by teaching in broadly chronological periods that a child's sense of relative historical time can develop at all. Fortunately, many teachers are willing to vary the usual treatment by taking projects and themes, and more radical proposals have recently been made which suggest that the essential task of the history teacher is to teach the 'mode of enquiry' of the subject, or to develop specific 'historical' skills, which, it is suggested, would do much to counteract the excessive emphasis on factual information which external examinations also tend at present to encourage.[20]

Some of these proposals are of equal interest when considering teaching methods in institutions of higher education. In this sphere also, much attention is being given to teaching techniques. The proper function of the lecture, and the best ways of conducting seminars and tutorials, are currently being examined and we may conclude by considering how far the teaching of history of education is taking account of these developments. The large number of elements in the courses given to intending teachers and the large number of students involved means that in most colleges and university departments of education much reliance is placed on the general lecture, sometimes with the aid of closed-circuit television. The lecture has traditionally been used to give an outline of a subject, as the basis for further reading by the student. An alternative and no doubt better way of using the lecture is to break new ground or to stimulate interest. This usually implies that the students have made some study of the subject beforehand, or that sufficient books are available for them to fill in the background for themselves by private reading. In many colleges the supply of suitable books is inadequate, so that students perforce have to derive their knowledge from the lectures alone. Indeed, in many places the general lecture is found in its least valuable form – addressed to a large audience, covering a very wide subject in a short number of weeks.

Similarly, seminars and tutorials are of little value unless the students have themselves read and thought about the subjects to be discussed, and a written essay is still probably the best method for the student to organise his material and for the tutor to ensure that the subject has been fully understood. This in turn involves generous staffing ratios, time for reading and writing, and an adequate supply of books. At present, the shortage of facilities has resulted in offering these more enlightened teaching methods to a minority only – for example, in the colleges to B.Ed. candidates, and in the university departments to those students who 'opt' to concentrate on the history of education instead of one of the other disciplines of education, or among the relatively small number of practising teachers reading for a diploma or higher degree in education.

It is difficult, therefore, not to conclude that, in the present situation, with the majority of students receiving only a limited number of general lectures on the history of education, the impact of the subject is seriously reduced. It is to be hoped that the restructuring of the system of teacher education now under consideration will provide better opportunities for the study of the history of education, and the other disciplines of education, than have been generally available hitherto. When the various disciplines are more fully established, it should be possible to devise courses which aim at studying their interaction in more detail, and to devise common courses in education which, unlike those in the past, will provide intellectual stimulation and coherence as well as width of range.

References

1   See, further, Burston, W. H., and Thompson, D. (eds.), *Studies in the Nature and Teaching of History*. Routledge and Kegan Paul, 1967, pp. 65 f.

2   Sutherland, G., 'The study of the history of education', in *History*, Vol. LIV, No. 180, Feb. 1969, pp. 49 f.

3   Charlton, K., in History of Education Society, *History, Sociology and Education*. Methuen, 1971, ch. 4.

4   Whitbread, N., 'History of education within the education course', in *Education for Teaching*, Summer 1967, p. 38.

5   Simon, B., 'The history of education', in Tibble, J. W. (ed.), *The Study of Education*. Routledge and Kegan Paul, 1966, p. 105.

6   Richardson, J. A. S., 'The content of three-year courses in the principles of education', in *Education for Teaching*, Summer 1968, pp. 53 f.

7   Nash, P. (ed.), *History and Education*. New York, Random House, 1970, p. 3.

8   See Fines, J. D., *The Teaching of History in the United Kingdom. A Select Bibliography*, The Historical Association, 1969. For recent examples, see Sturley, D.M., *The Study of History*, Longmans, 1969; Thomson, D., *The Aims of History*, Thames and Hudson, 1969; and Marwick, A., *The Nature of History*, Macmillan, 1970.

9   Cox, C. B., and Dyson, A. E. (eds.), *Black Paper Three*. The Critical Quarterly Society, 1970, p. 69.

10 Elton, G. R., 'What sort of history should we teach?', in Ballard, M. (ed.), *New Movements in the Study and Teaching of History*. Temple Smith, 1970, p. 226, p. 225.

11 Perkin, H. (ed.), *History. An Introduction for the Intending Student*. Routledge and Kegan Paul, 1970, pp. 12-13.

12 *Ibid.*

13 Ballard, *op. cit.*

14 Oakeshott, M., *Experience and its Modes*. Cambridge, 1933.

15 Burston, W. H., *Principles of History Teaching*. Methuen, 1963, p. 35.

16 See, for example, Shafer, B. C., *et al.*, *Historical Study in the West*. New York, Appleton-Century-Crofts, 1968.

17 Plumb, J. H. (ed.), *Crisis in the Humanities*. Penguin Books, 1964. Quotations from pp. 36-7 and 43.

18 Stone, L., in *Past and Present*, 42, February 1969, p. 69.

19 For a review of the literature on the history of education to 1966, see Simon in Tibble, *op.cit.*, pp. 112 f. For later books and current research see the *Bulletins* of the History of Education Society from 1968.

20 See Lamont, W., 'The uses and abuses of examinations' in Ballard, *op.cit.*, pp. 192 f., and Booth, M. B., *History Betrayed?* Longmans, 1969.

E

Psychology of Education

PAPER 3

William Anthony

WHAT IS PSYCHOLOGY OF EDUCATION?

Psychology of education is psychology done with the intention of improving our knowledge of education, and probably with the intention of improving education itself.

Psychology may be defined as the study (or the science) of mind (or of behaviour). The presence of alternatives in the definition indicates uncertainty about the nature of the subject. In this section, I shall examine some opinions on what psychology is, and especially Professor Ben Morris's[1] opinions on what kind of psychology can contribute to the study of education. The second and third sections consider the questions 'What is its justification in the education of teachers?' and 'How should it be taught?'

When the psychologist William James talked to school-teachers about psychology, he told them that 'psychology is a science, and teaching is an art',[2] but when he wrote for students of psychology, he told them that psychology 'is no science, it is only the hope of a science'.[3] No doubt James considered that it was useful for teachers to believe that psychology was a science, and useful for psychologists to believe that it was not. However calm and efficient the psychologist may contrive to appear when in view of the teachers, behind closed doors he must struggle to prop up the creaking façade.

It is many years since James wrote that psychology was only the hope of a science, and some psychologists would now claim that the hope has been fulfilled, that psychology is now a science with established theories, a vast amount of information, sophisticated methods of research, and applications in many walks of life. Other psychologists would claim that the hope has faded, that it has become clear that psychology can never become a science, that scientific methods have yielded nothing worthwhile in psychology, and that the whole enterprise is an even bigger sham than it was in James's time. However, Thomson moderately argues that 'the story . . . is one of modest but positive progress',[4] and most psychologists would probably be happy to settle for such a verdict.

Despite any doubts, students of psychology are commonly invited to think of it as the *science of behaviour*. (Sometimes this notion of psychology is called 'behaviourism', but at other times 'behaviourism' is restricted to theories of 'conditioning'; to call someone a 'behaviourist' is often to convey an insult of uncertain meaning.) The term 'science' is used to imply that psychology is based on empirical data – that is, on information gained in observation by sight, hearing, or the other senses. The term 'behaviour' is used because behaviour is reckoned to be more observable and less mysterious than mind. It may be doubted whether mind is observable, but it is obvious that we can often observe someone's behaviour (that is, what he says and does), and that his observable behaviour is usually some indication of his state of mind. Advances in physiological techniques increase our ability to observe the internal behaviour of the brain and other bodily functions. Furthermore, a person's conscious experience *may* be regarded as behaviour which he alone can observe (a somewhat heterodox view, because science in general seeks objective observation where there is agreement between different observers). The definition of psychology as the science of behaviour does not solve the psychological and philosophical problems of mind, but it does help us to ignore or cut violently through a number of problems (as has been done in this paragraph) in order to attend to the behaviour which can be observed.

In aligning itself with science, psychology has generally

sought to attain a clear relationship between theory and empirical reality. Theories (ideas, hypotheses) are to be tested by experience (not necessarily by experiment, which is a special form of experience). The orthodox view of psychology includes Popper's requirement that 'it must be possible for an empirical scientific system to be refuted by experience'.[5] The following simple argument will suggest what Popper is getting at. Consider the statement, 'It will rain, or be fine, or something.' Such a statement is scientifically uninformative: it cannot be tested, or checked; no observation could be inconsistent with it, or refute it, or cast doubt on it. A more complex example from psychology would be: 'Our life is spent in anxiety.' It is not clear whether this could be tested; if someone is obviously anxious then this apparently confirms the statement, but if someone shows no sign of anxiety then this does not refute it, because it could be claimed that the person was superficially calm but anxious underneath. It could even be said that observed calm casts no doubt at all on the statement that our life is spent in anxiety, because the statement is too vague to be clearly related to what can be observed. In orthodox psychology, we must be very suspicious of theoretical language which is not clearly related to experience. Popper[6] comments disparagingly on the apparent irrefutability of Adler's and Freud's theories. Orthodox psychology shares Popper's distrust of these (psychoanalytic) theories and of other theories which are not falsifiable by evidence.[7,8]

Now it must be admitted that, in the practice of orthodox psychology, one empirical observation by itself would not usually be allowed to 'refute' (disprove, falsify) a theory even if it appeared to do so. More likely, such an observation is said to be 'inconsistent' with the theory, or to 'fail to confirm' it, or to 'cast doubt' on it. A coherent system of ideas may survive many apparent refutations (compare Kuhn[9]). The principle remains, however, that a theory must be subject to the check of experience. Experience is the check, the constraint, that orthodox psychology claims to impose upon itself as its justification of its ideas.

It should be evident that orthodox psychology, when applied to education, will be eager to test children, that is, to put children in standard situations in order to record how they behave in these situations. The child's recorded behaviour (his 'score', perhaps, on a variety of 'tests') will usually be taken as indicating his state of mind (his perceptions, abilities, understandings, skills, memories, character, attitudes, needs, personality, or what have you) and the definitions of these terms for research purposes is of course a large part of orthodox psychology's job. *The Taxonomy of Educational Objectives*, of Bloom, Krathwohl and others[10, 11] is a classic product of the orthodox psychology of education, in which the sustained attempt is made to classify states of mind which may be thought educationally desirable, and to define these mental states in terms of observable behaviour. A term like 'comprehension' can thus be given meaning in terms of performance on a defined class of tests. This should facilitate communication between teachers, examiners, and researchers. (In working out such schemes, the dangers of dogmatism, and the claims of ordinary language and of every man's values, must naturally be borne in mind.)

It will be evident also that orthodox psychology of education will wish to carry out empirical research, that is, to arrange for observations of behaviour to be made which are capable of testing ideas concerning educational problems. Most of what goes by the name of 'educational research' is of this sort, though it is not all done by 'psychologists'. Books edited by Gage,[12] Butcher,[13] and Butcher and Pont[14] contain convenient reviews and bibliographies of educational research of this orthodox type.

Revolt against orthodox psychology
Naturally, an orthodoxy has its opponents; indeed, it is the opponents who make us aware of the orthodoxy. In the *Bulletin* of the British Psychological Society, Joynson[15] argues that psychology, in attempting to become a science, has retreated from much of its proper concerns, and has gained little; 'perhaps,

however, the time is coming when broader and more appropriate ideals will prevail'.[16] In the same issue of the *Bulletin*, Hudson[17] claims that his best students resist confinement to the empirical tradition in psychology. He urges academic psychologists to meet the students half-way, to find some new paradigm, though he confesses himself unable to suggest what this new paradigm might be.

Whereas Joynson and Hudson ache for something they know not what, Morris[18] knows what he wants in psychology and, what is more, he thinks it exists already. Morris is concerned, as we are, with the contribution of psychology to the study of education; therefore we shall examine his views with particular interest. Following Macmurray,[19, 20] Morris distinguishes three forms of thought, which he names the mechanistic, the organic, and the personal. Briefly, the mechanistic form of thought in psychology considers man as a machine, without purposes and without individuality. The organic form of thought in psychology considers man as a unique isolable individual with purposes. The personal form of thought – and this is the form which Morris is concerned to advocate – considers man as a person intrinsically related to others. 'At the level of the personal, education is neither doing things *to* people nor *for* them, but *with* them.'[21] The teacher and student are to be in relation of mutuality, each learning from the other. Since educational thought must be in the form of the personal, psychology must also be in, or if possible transformed into, the personal form, if it is to be relevant to education.

Now, we could argue that what is positive in these three forms of thought has already been absorbed into orthodox psychology. We could argue that, in orthodox psychology, *a*) man is regarded as a machine; *b*) man is regarded as a unique, purposive, machine on the analogy of a unique problem-solving computer fed with unique data; and *c*) man is regarded as intrinsically related to others, as a computer is intrinsically related (through the transmission of data) to the people or machines who/which feed it and feed upon it.

But Morris's exposition shows that he is not arguing for a

computer-based psychology of education, or anything like that! He picks his sources from a vast field, including anthropology, mythology, literature, and ethology, as well as much of orthodox psychology, but his most prominent recommendations[22] are of psychoanalytic writings and especially the work of Harry Guntrip and Erik H. Erikson. Has Morris thus shown the way to the broader ideals for which Joynson pines? Has Morris found the paradigm for which Hudson is looking?

'What is required,' Morris writes, 'is the cultivation of the kind of sympathy through which we are able in imagination to *identify* with others, to experience something of their joys and sorrows, their problems, failures and achievements. Moreover we have to learn to do this without surrendering our own identity and independence. This cultivation of the power of detached but sympathetic identification lies at the heart of making the study of psychology truly personal.'[23] Note that Morris's 'identification' is to be 'detached'; each of us is to be at one with another, and yet each is also to be cut off from the other.

How might such a detached identification be cultivated? Morris tells us that in an education course it may be done primarily through studies of children and adults very different from oneself. Here is a rather more extended description of the cultivation of 'identification' in insurance salesmen: 'There were lengthy group sessions, where Bernie and his men picked over the techniques of their craft. They practised "sincere smiles" in front of mirrors – in later, more opulent days, training films were made on the finer points of smiling – and they practised "firm handshakes" on each other. Cornfeld impressed upon them that they should always try to sit next to a prospect, rather than across the table from him, where it would be harder to "win his confidence".'[24] To echo Morris: at the level of the personal, insurance salesmanship is neither doing things *to* people nor *for* them, but *with* them. So what is the difference between an insurance salesman and a teacher? Obviously there are similarities and differences between the two occupations, and there is room for controversy concerning the type of training in personal relations that is appropriate to each. Some empirical research,[25] which has received a guardedly favourable review,[26] has obtained results suggesting that 'empathy', 'non-possessive warmth' and 'genuineness' (terms apparently similar to Morris's 'detached but sympathetic identification') are effective in counselling and psychotherapy. But this research is apparently an effort in orthodox psychology; I find no suggestion in Morris that such research should be done.

If we refer to the psychoanalytic writers prominently recommended by Morris, we find that Guntrip[27] and Erikson[28] both imply that the psychoanalyst tests his interpretation against his further experience; but they do not go on to explain how this testing is done. The orthodox psychologist, with orthodox distrust of psychoanalysis, would argue that the psychoanalyst does not really test his interpretation because he does not test it against objectively perceived behaviour. What is the validity of supposed 'intuition', 'empathy', 'identification', and so on? Such terms are to be distrusted unless the 'intuiter' is concerned to check his intuition against 'objective' perception (that is, the agreement in perception of different observers).

Any reasonable intellectual enquiry must seek to check its ideas against such 'evidence' as may be judged appropriate. History[29] does so; so does literary criticism;[30] so does orthodox psychology. Psychoanalysis has often been called unscientific, but the more damaging objection against it would be that it were unreasonable.[31] It does not seem that there is a reasonable method whereby psychoanalysts check their ideas.

Professor Morris advocates a very broad psychology of education, based primarily on the psychoanalytic ideas of Guntrip and Erikson, but he emphasises that it is to be a disciplined study.[32] However, since it is doubtful whether there is a discipline (a method of enquiry) in psychoanalysis, it seems that the proposed broadened psychology would not be disciplined at its psychoanalytic core, although the discipline of orthodoxy might be tacked on somehow at the outside. The further requirement for a teacher of psychology to be familiar with half a dozen fields of arts and social sciences, and to be capable of integrating them into an intelligible picture, is unlikely to be fulfilled, so that such a course does not seem to be a practical possibility.

We see then that there is some disappointment with orthodox psychology and some desire for an alternative view of the subject. The great strength of orthodox psychology is that it keeps in contact with reality by subjecting its ideas to empirical testing; it also extends its contact with reality by devising new methods of observation. It seems to me that, in the proposals for an alternative psychology, such as by Morris and by 'humanistic' psychology,[33] the 'reasonableness' of orthodox psychology has been given up (except as an optional extra), without any other sort of reasonableness being substituted. Perhaps a reasonable (disciplined) alternative will emerge; but this is the promise of the future. The remainder of this paper will concentrate on the orthodox psychology of education, on the grounds that this is the only reasonable psychology of education that we have.

WHY INCLUDE PSYCHOLOGY OF EDUCATION IN THE EDUCATION OF TEACHERS?

In the preceding section, the view was developed that (orthodox) psychology of education is justified as a reasonable study by the fact that it seeks to check its ideas against observations of behaviour. The point was also made that most educational research is psychological in this sense.

In my opinion, the justification for the various parts of a course in the psychology of education will be different according to the different sorts of empirical data which are relevant to each part. The data relevant to a typical course in the psychology of education may be divided into four sections as follows: assessment, research on background conditions, research on teaching, and informal experience. This is not a statement of what should be taught, or of the order in which anything should be taught, and it does not imply that empirical data should take precedence over the ideas to which they are relevant. It is only a rough classification of data for the purpose of discussing the justification for teaching the various parts of the course. Each class of data will be taken in turn.

Assessment

Here we have in mind the assessment of a child's (or, more rarely, a teacher's) abilities, anxieties, attitudes, attractiveness, ... The list of possible words is endless; their meanings overlap somewhat, and vary in precision. Nevertheless, assessment is the main function of an examiner, and a principal function of a professional 'educational psychologist' (a clinician) in Britain.[34] *The Psychological Assessment of Mental and Physical Handicaps*, by Mittler and others,[35] and *The Taxonomy of Educational Objectives*[10, 11] cover a large part of the enormous field of assessment. Any given method of assessment is open to doubt, but the 'psychometrist' has various criteria by which a method may be judged. These criteria tend to be grouped under the terms 'reliability' and 'validity', terms which can be applied with or without due caution.

There is no denying that pupils are assessed by various methods, more or less technical, at various times in their school life. Recommendations and decisions follow from such assessments. Teachers may be involved in communication with psychologists and examiners, and it is evident that a teacher will be more able to contribute to, and make use of, assessments, recommendations, and decisions, if he has some acquaintance with the technical concepts and problems. This more obviously applies to teachers of children designated as 'handicapped' in some way, and to teachers who have become involved in newer forms of secondary-school examination, or who have otherwise become involved in problems of assessment, as in the research reported by Eggleston and Kerr.[36] It should be noted that there are special problems in 'continuous assessment', and also where students are assessed for work done in groups, and where 'social' and 'personal' (as distinct from intellectual) qualities are considered to be important educational goals. The adoption of wide educational aims should imply a concern for wide and credible methods of assessment. The teacher who ignores these problems may be too easily accused of evasion of responsibility. If he relies on his unaided intuitive judgment, his assessments lack credibility. If teachers leave assessment entirely to non-teachers, they diminish their own profession. For these reasons, an introduction to methods of assessment should be included in the education of teachers.

However, there are further arguments. The development of methods of assessment of educational objectives should clarify the objectives themselves and thus should encourage the development of more effective teaching (he who wills the end wills the means); there is a concomitant danger that difficulties of assessment would lead to undue *restriction* of objectives and thus to poorer teaching, and this must be guarded against. Incidentally, students of education may be interested to reflect on the problems of assessing *them*. The findings of low agreement between assessments should interest them, although some colleges may think it wise to keep this secret.[37] An interesting possibility is in the more deliberate use of instant-by-instant assessment of pupil attention and understanding, for example, by teacher's interpretation of facial expression,[38] or, futuristically, by psychophysiological indices, such as heart-beat[39] instantly displayed for the teacher's information. A final reason for the importance of methods of assessment as a topic in teacher education is that these techniques are relevant to some topics in the philosophy and sociology of education, and are fundamental to the types of research to be considered below.

Research into background conditions

By 'background conditions', I mean the conditions which the teacher has to accept, at least for the time being. Of course, this depends on how powerful the teacher is, but background conditions may be taken to include the teacher's own age, sex, and family background; his pupils' age, sex, and family background (assuming that the teacher is committed to a particular set of pupils); teacher's and pupils' abilities and personalities (so far as these are not under the teacher's control); the local and national educational and social systems (not changeable by the teacher in his rôle as worker in the school).

The meaning of 'research into background conditions' will be clearer when contrasted with 'research into teaching'. By 'research into teaching' I mean research into the effects of 'optional conditions', that is to say conditions which *are* under the teacher's control. The optional conditions include much of the teacher's behaviour, including (to some extent) the manner and content of his speech, his method of teaching, and the general course of events in the space and time for which he is responsible.

Now, research into background conditions may tell the teacher what to *expect*, but it cannot of itself tell the teacher what to *do* (because it does not investigate the effect of what he does, it only investigates the effect of things that he cannot do anything about). Research on 'child development' is mostly research into background conditions. Many attributes are found to develop – that is, they change with age, age being the background condition. For instance, Piaget and his followers have reported many such relationships.[40] It would be a naïve interpretation of this research to suppose that age itself, the mere passing of time, was the cause of the changes observed. Piaget's[41] interpretation cannot be summarised here, but one particular notion of Piaget's is often emphasised: the notion that the child acquires 'concrete operations' by *activity*. Now, related research into teaching does not confirm this view; Sigel and Hooper's[42] collection of research reports include several experiments where the child was passive (except for speech), yet where training was effective. Yet in a chapter apparently intended to review the research presented, Hooper[43] ignores the research and instead emphasises Piaget's view that activity upon material objects is necessary.

Similarly, many students are so impressed by the volume and variety of Piagetian research that they fail to notice the fact that it does not test ideas about teaching at all; the comparatively small amount of Piaget-inspired research which does test ideas about how to teach tends to be ignored. There is, in fact, a systematic tendency for research into background conditions to give rise to ideas about teaching; those who are engaged or interested in the research naturally wish to propose that some particular type of action should be taken, and may not test the action first.

The justification for including research into background conditions, and related ideas, in a course of psychology of education is therefore rather more shaky than is commonly supposed. However, there are arguments to be noted. The material tells the teacher what he may expect to find in, say, 'the six year old', 'the lower-working-class adolescent', and thus prepares him for his future experience, particularly if he is prepared for deviations, even perhaps among whole classes of children, from the supposed norms. Much of the material has 'human interest'; furthermore, if students are led to consider the relation between a child's present behaviour and his life as a whole, including his past experience of home and school, then this should foster calm and humane attitudes to children who have annoying tendencies.

Research into background conditions may also properly suggest the desirability of various courses of action, provided that the student is aware that the research has not tested the effect of the course of action which it suggests. Research into background conditions often introduces new forms of assessment, brings to light previously unnoticed deficiencies, and creates new educational objectives in the minds of teachers.

Research into teaching

As previously explained, 'research into teaching' is used here to mean research investigating the effects of teaching-methods and of other conditions which can be controlled by teachers. It is therefore the sort of research which could be expected to tell the teacher how to teach. Or, in view of the uniqueness of each situation, this type of research could be expected to provide sound 'guidance' or 'suggestions' for teaching.

However, this research very often yields doubtful and inconclusive results. Thouless, in his *Map of Educational Research*, concludes that 'in spite of the increasing volume of educational research carefully carried out, its impact on teaching practice remains relatively small'.[44] Stephens[45] points, with some documentary evidence, to the large number of negative results obtained in research on teaching. The various conditions of teaching generally seem to be equally effective; the differences in effect are either statistically nonsignificant, or else mutually inconsistent.

According to Campbell and Stanley,[46] in the 1920s there was a wave of mistaken enthusiasm in America for experimental research on teaching. ('Experimental' here means that the researcher has some control over the conditions which are being studied.) But 'when, in fact, experiments often proved to be tedious, equivocal, of undependable replicability, and to confirm pre-scientific wisdom, the overoptimistic grounds on which experimentation had been justified were undercut, and a disillusioned rejection or neglect took place'.[47] This wave of pessimism began in about 1935; educationists turned from research to essay-writing. Campbell and Stanley (in 1963) believed that 'we must instill in our students the expectation of tedium and disappointment and the duty of thorough persistence, by now so well achieved in the biological and physical sciences' and that experimentation is to be justified not as a panacea but as 'the only available route to cumulative progress',[48] 'the only way of establishing a cumulative tradition in which improvements can be introduced without the danger of a faddish discard of old wisdom in favour of inferior novelties'.[49]

Much has been made here of disappointment. However, it is the educational researcher who has most cause for disappointment, not the teacher. If one treatment (one method of teaching, and so on) were found to be decisively more effective than another, then indeed some teachers might reasonably be pressed to change their methods, perhaps much against their will and on the basis of 'mere statistics'. As things are, the teacher may reasonably choose the method which seems to work best for himself. The publication of indecisive results actually helps to free the teacher from the pressures of educational fashion.

However, it is unlikely that the teacher of psychology will rest content with this interpretation of research data. Researchers themselves, and reviewers of research, frequently draw positive, or tentatively positive, conclusions from the results which they or others have obtained. One sort of conclusion which is often drawn is that, for one particular group of pupils, one treatment is more suitable than another treatment. Such a conclusion may arise as follows. Research into teaching conditions often includes an investigation of what we have called 'background conditions' as well, so that there are a great many ways in which the pupils may be classified (by age, by sex, by ability, by personality, and so on); it is thus likely that even by pure chance some group of pupils would be found to have done distinctly better under one treatment than under another. Such effects of 'interaction' (as it is called) between treatment variables and background variables become labelled 'statistically significant' by the processes of statistical analysis even when they have arisen by pure chance. This is well known to researchers. One way of dealing with the difficulty is to look for consistent effects of interaction among different pieces of research. My impression is that effects of interaction are not in general consistent; that is to say, the search for generalisations about what sort of method is more suitable for what sort of pupil has been no more successful than the search for simple differences in the effectiveness of the methods *without* regard to pupil differences.

One general difficulty is that there is no obvious discipline in the reviewing of research results. Faced with a mass of confusing reports, some reviewers seem to feel free to draw whatever conclusions they wish. Their summary can then be quoted by others: 'Smith, after reviewing 17 studies of the effect of X compared with the effect of Y, concluded that in general X tended to be the more effective, except for middle-class girls' may conceal the fact that a reader looking at Smith's review could not conceive how Smith managed to arrive at that particular summary conclusion, and might wish, on the basis of the same 17 studies, to come out with the conclusion that there was some tendency for Y to be more effective except where the teachers were introverted or were born in Scotland.

An example of a reasonably disciplined approach to research evidence will now be given. Kersh and Wittrock[50] reviewed experiments on learning by discovery. Their review was interpreted by me to imply a testable hypothesis, which may be simply expressed as follows: learning by discovery of principles is a relatively good way of teaching students how to discover more principles of the same kind, but this depends upon the students discovering a sufficient (unspecified) proportion of the first set of principles, the ones which they are supposed to discover in the learning session. It occurred to me that sufficient data had now been published to allow this hypothesis to be tested statistically.

Consequently, seven relevant experimental comparisons were found in the research literature. The hypothesis was confirmed by the finding of a significant correlation between learning-by-discovery students' success in their learning sessions and their success (relative to equivalent didactically-taught groups) on the test of ability to discover more principles. In these experiments, the discovery method was found to pay off provided that the initial success in the learning session was more than 50 per cent in the given learning-by-discovery group. Thus, this little body of research literature, when examined statistically as a whole, is found to be internally consistent in supporting the hypothesis derived from Kersh and Wittrock, and in supporting the common notion among teachers who use discovery methods, that the teacher must provide for success in discovery. (However, the advantage for discovery methods, when it occurred in these experiments, was generally very slight.) The point of the preceding example is to illustrate the desirability of a disciplined search for consistency *between* research studies as well as for consistency *within* any given research study. This is particularly true of research into teaching, because of the prevalence of apparently inconsistent results and the consequent pressure towards unjustifiable generalisations.

Hilgard, in 1956, included at the end of his authoritative *Theories of Learning*[51] a list of 14 practical principles of learning and teaching, arising from experimentation, with which he thought that there would be general agreement. Ten years later, in a new edition, the same writer[52] presented an adapted list of 20 practical principles, with which again he expected general agreement. This new list omits four, and radically alters three, of the original list of 14, so that only half the original principles remain. Such devastation indicates the flexibility of our science; it also confirms that we cannot place much reliance on psychological principles of learning and teaching.

The justification for including research into teaching, and its associated ideas, in the education of teachers is that the ideas, when suitably constrained by the research, are the reasonable and realistic notions of the effectiveness of various teaching methods and other teacher-controlled conditions. The actual results of such research tend to be inconclusive, but if the research were ignored then all general recommendations about teaching would go unchecked by reality; as we have pointed out, the very failure of research, *if it is known* to him and to others, protects the teacher's freedom of action, and accords him a professional dignity which would otherwise be diminished.

Informal data

The category of informal data is mentioned here, not because it provides any special justification for teaching the (orthodox) psychology of education, but because it forms an important part of the data and must not be forgotten.

Some facts are so obvious in ordinary life that they do not need to be demonstrated by research. Case-studies (relatively 'informal') have intrinsic interest and serve as concrete illustrations of principles. Lecturers commonly draw upon their own unsystematic personal experience; the student may be

F

encouraged to draw upon *his* experience and to reflect upon it carefully. Some students are too ready to generalise from their own experience; others are too reluctant to recall and reflect on it at all. For the teacher of psychology to ignore the student's own experience is to imply: 'Oh, you and your life don't count, I am telling you about what psychologists have found out.' In some ways, a student may properly be more certain of his own experience than he is of all the data which are reported to him by others. But we can point out to him, in general and with respect to the particular case, the possibility of misperception, misremembering, and misinterpretation, depending on the circumstances.

In this category of informal data we may also include all forms of interpersonal experience set up in the education course itself. Here there is a special problem of the effect of institutional bias upon the experience. The experience of a student in (say) a discussion group, or indeed his whole life while he is on the course, is likely to be affected by the values of the teachers and students on the course. It is therefore likely to be unrepresentative of society at large. Presumably we do not wish, by over-emphasis on the student's current personal experience, to teach him a psychology which is actually only a psychology of those with whom he happens to be in contact at the time. Experience in schools should of course be some corrective to this, unless it too is selected to confirm some institutional bias.

Hannam, Smyth and Stephenson[53] report a project in which students (prospective teachers) were brought into prolonged weekly informal contact with early school leavers attending a comprehensive school; each student was 'attached' to two or three children for one academic year. It seems that this project is of the sort which might provide something of what Professor Morris advocates. The subjectivity and individuality of the data would exclude it from orthodox psychology as at present conceived. But there is opportunity for 'discipline' in the student's analysis of his experience, and scope for any reasonable testing of ideas as the student tries out new approaches with the children and gets to know them. We may hope that this is an area in which reasonable thought can flourish, and into which psychology might fruitfully break out of its orthodoxy.

The preceding rough classification of material by type of relevant data has enabled us to refer to very large areas of subject-matter which seem to share similar justifications for their inclusion in teacher education. The classes of data overlap, so that in many cases the inclusion of one section of material could be justified by drawing upon arguments which were proposed for different classes of data.

We have argued that the psychology of education cannot tell teachers how to teach, but that there are nevertheless many reasons for its inclusion in the education of teachers, where it is fairly widely respected. It is to be hoped that as information and sophistication accumulate, respect for the subject will increase.

HOW SHOULD PSYCHOLOGY OF EDUCATION BE TAUGHT?

I wish to consider the contrast between two extreme methods of teaching the psychology of education: first, the action-oriented method, and, second, the reason-oriented method. (My attention was drawn to this contrast at a very interesting conference on the teaching of psychology, held at the C. F. Mott College of Education, Liverpool, in April 1971.)

In the first method, the main emphasis would be on expounding principles for action by the student in his teaching practice and in his future work as a teacher. In some sense, the lecturer tells the student how to teach; he attempts to ensure that the student understands how to apply the principles; and he may also watch him to see that he does apply the principles in practice. Micro-teaching[54] could be useful here.

In the second method, the main emphasis would be in expounding what is known or believed or doubted in the psychology of education, and how it is that we come to know or believe or doubt it. In the first method, the aim is to present a convincing system of thought which will impel the student into action and give him confidence in what he is doing and thinking as a teacher. In the second method, the aim is to display the content and nature of psychology, in order that he shall have confidence only so far as confidence is justifiable in the light of experience.

The action-oriented method is implied in some impressive work of Stones and Anderson.[55] These authors report a study of objectives in the teaching of psychology to student teachers. Tutors in psychology, students, and teachers were asked to evaluate 50 possible objectives. In the result, there was broad agreement between the three groups. The most highly valued objective was that the student 'be willing to modify his teaching methods to allow for the varying needs of individual children'; the least valued objective was to 'be able to state the most important features of Freudian and neo-Freudian psychology'. In general, the most valued objectives[56] could be summarised in the words, 'be able and willing to teach well', and the least valued objectives[57] could be summarised as 'know what some psychologists and statisticians think and do'.

As a result of considering their data and other material, Stones and Anderson write: 'It seems to us that a statement of objectives in a course in educational psychology for student teachers should have as its central focus the need for students to acquire a sound grasp of the psychological principles relating to human learning and teaching and the ability to apply them to classroom situations.'[58] The authors maintain this focus in their system of objectives, which occupies a large part of their book. They do not state what they consider the 'psychological principles' to be. This would have been unwise, for (as we have inferred from our consideration of Hilgard's work) a psychological principle of learning and teaching has a 50 per cent chance of radical alteration or disappearance within ten years. But the reference to unspecified principles recurs throughout the system.

The intention, then, is to require the student to be able to recall and apply a very large number of coherent principles relating to learning and teaching. There is not, in the system of objectives, any requirement that he should be able to criticise the principles or be able to bring evidence for or against them. This would tend to reduce his commitment to the system, and might make him confused and less confident. He is not required to know that the principles which he is being taught are somewhat different from those which have been taught to others or from those which will be taught to his successors. It is a consequence of the Stones-Anderson system that if we find that the student has somehow acquired a taste for principles other than the official ones set for him, we must strive to persuade him to accept these, or else he will fail our course. No doubt the system could be made to operate smoothly by 1984.

The contrasted method of teaching psychology is the reason-oriented method, where the emphasis is on the critical appreciation of ideas in the light of research and of other experience. This emphasis is advocated by Thouless,[59] and by three writers, Peter Robinson,[60] Peter Renshaw,[61] and Eric Robinson,[62] in a recent 'critique of teacher education'. However, we must add that the three last-named writers are not concerned specifically with the psychology course, but with the student's course as a whole. The B.P.S. and A.T.C.D.E. joint report in 1962, *Teaching Educational Psychology in Training Colleges*,[63] appears to put approximately equal emphasis on action- and reason-oriented content.

There are three main objections to the reason-oriented type of course. First, it lacks coherence. This is true, in that we have no single adequate coherent view of 'man' that stands up to what we know of him. If we are to encourage students to use their reason, any one given view can be seen to be inadequate. However, we can impose some coherence in various ways. For instance, we can follow the development of the child from conception onwards. We can choose one or more theoretical positions (for study, not for passive acceptance); they could be developmental theories such as those of Erikson and Piaget, or they could be relatively age-free, such as Gagné's *The Conditions of Learning*[64] or 'communication theory'. (An advantage of communication theory is that it allows us to represent

interpersonal relations in the same terms as the *intra*personal
relations between perception, memory, response and so on; so
that overt and covert events in the whole classroom can be
conceived simultaneously.) We can also make use of the coherence of psychological methods of enquiry. But there is no
denying that one coherent and reasonable view (if it could be
achieved) would be more satisfactory.

The second objection is that critical thinking is too difficult.
I think this objection arises because the pieces of research or
thinking which the student may be asked to criticise have not
been graded for difficulty. If we take 'critical thinking' or
'research-mindedness' seriously as an objective then we should
not expect the student to begin on the first piece of relevant
material that 'comes up'; we must tailor the material to the
student's present level of sophistication and work from simple
to complex. For students to plan their own (real or imaginary)
piece of research can be a very useful exercise: in discussion,
problems of design can be raised, and solved or mitigated.

The third objection is that the reason-oriented method does
not give a clear guide to action. 'Psychology is a science, and
teaching is an art; and sciences never generate arts directly out
of themselves.'[65] Morris argues that psychology should become
an art; Stones and Anderson imply that teaching is a science;
both these ways of closing the gap seem to me illusory, for
reasons already mentioned. In an extremely reason-oriented
course of psychology, the teacher might refuse to allow any
mention of action. But in a more normal case, the teacher will
probably draw out 'implications' for action, or encourage
students to draw out such 'implications', from the ideas and
data, teacher or students suggesting how sure or doubtful the
implication is.

In some courses, the psychology teacher may be expected to
give plentiful guidance for action; in other courses, teaching
methods and other advice for action comes from other members of staff, and then the teacher of psychology could perform
a specific critical function of directing attention to criticism
and research data. Alternatively, he could direct his attention

entirely to matters outside the concern of other courses – for example, to social, emotional, or moral development. Here again, the reason-oriented method would require the critical evaluation of ideas and data.

In the first section of this paper, it was argued that the psychology of education, as a reasonable form of thought, subjects its ideas to the check of empirical reality. In the second section it was argued that psychology was justifiably included in the education of teachers for various reasons, including the teacher's interest in assessment, the formation of reasonable expectations from children, and the protection of the teacher's freedom in choice of teaching method, among other arguments which were and might have been given. It is possible to teach the (often dubious) conclusions of psychology without teaching the methods by which they are reached, and one cannot delve into the details every time; but a student can participate in psychology only so far as he is acquainted with the methods of its enquiry.

References

1   Morris, B., 'The contribution of psychology to the study of education', In J. W. Tibble (ed.), *The Study of Education*. Routledge and Kegan Paul, 1966.
2   James, W., *Talks to Teachers on Psychology and to Students on Some of Life's Ideals*. Longmans, 1904 (1st edition, 1899), p. 7.
3   James, W., *Text Book of Psychology: Briefer Course*. Macmillan, no date (1st edition, 1892), p. 468.
4   Thomson, R., *The Pelican History of Psychology*. Penguin, 1968, p. 431.
5   Popper, K. R., *The Logic of Scientific Discovery*. Hutchinson, 1959, p. 41.
6   Popper, K. R., *Conjectures and Refutations*. Routledge and Kegan Paul, 1963, pp. 34-8.
7   Hall, C. S. and Lindzey, G., 'The relevance of Freudian psychology and related viewpoints for the social sciences', in G. Lindzey and E. Aronson (ed.), *The Handbook of Social Psychology*, 2nd Edn., Vol. I. Reading, Mass., Addison-Wesley, 1968, p. 287.
8   Wright, D. S. and others, *Introducing Psychology: an Experimental Approach*. Penguin, 1970, p. 19.
9   Kuhn, T. S., *The Structure of Scientific Revolutions*. Chicago, Ill., University of Chicago Press, 2nd edition, 1970, p. 146.

10 Bloom, B. S. (ed.), *Taxonomy of Educational Objectives, Handbook 1: Cognitive Domain*. Longmans, 1956.

11 Krathwohl, D. R., Bloom, B. S., and Masia, B. B., *Taxonomy of Educational Objectives, Handbook 2: Affective Domain*. Longmans, 1964.

12 Gage, N. L. (ed.), *Handbook of Research on Teaching*. Chicago, Ill., Rand McNally, 1963.

13 Butcher, H. J. (ed.), *Educational Research in Britain* 1. University of London Press, 1968.

14 Butcher, H. J., and Pont, H. B. (ed.), *Educational Research in Britain* 2,. University of London Press, 1970.

15 Joynson, R. B., 'The breakdown of modern psychology', in *Bull. Br. psychol. Soc.*, *23*, 1970, pp. 261-9.

16 *Ibid.*, p. 269.

17 Hudson, L., 'The choice of Hercules', *Bull. Br. psychol. Soc.*, *23*, 1970 pp. 287-92.

18 Morris, B., *op. cit.*

19 Macmurray, J., *The Self as Agent*. Faber and Faber, 1957.

20 Macmurray, J., *Persons in Relation*. Faber and Faber, 1961.

21 Morris, B., *op. cit.*, p. 149.

22 *Ibid.*, pp. 152, 154.

23 *Ibid.*, p. 170.

24 Raw, C., Page, B., and Hodgson, G., *Do You Sincerely Want To Be Rich?* André Deutsch, 1971. (Quotation from extract in *The Sunday Times*, 4 April 1971, p. 34.)

25 Truax, C. B., and Carkhuff, R. R., *Toward Effective Counselling and Psychotherapy*. Chicago, Ill., Aldine, 1967.

26 Shapiro, D. A., 'Empathy, warmth and genuineness in psychotherapy', in *Br. J. soc. clin. Psychol.*, *8*, 1969, pp. 350-61.

27 Guntrip, H., *Schizoid Phenomena, Object-Relations and the Self*. Hogarth, 1968, pp. 370, 373.

28 Erikson, E. H., *Insight and Responsibility*. New York, Norton, 1964, p. 80.

29 Gallie, W. B., *Philosophy and the Historical Understanding*. Chatto and Windus, 1964, pp. 73-4.

30 Casey, J., *The Language of Criticism*. Methuen, 1966, pp. 22, 175, 176.

31 Farrell, B. A., 'Psychoanalytic theory', *New Society*, 20 June 1963, reprinted in Lee, S. G. M. and Herbert, M. (ed.), *Freud and Psychology*. Penguin, 1970, pp. 19-28.

32 Morris, B., *op. cit.*, pp. 171, 172.

33 Bugental, J. F. T. (ed.), *Challenges of Humanistic Psychology*. New York, McGraw-Hill, 1967.

34 Summerfield, A. and others, *Psychologists in Education Services*. H.M.S.O., 1968, pp. 18, 114.

35 Mittler, P. (ed.), *The Psychological Assessment of Mental and Physical Handicaps*. Methuen, 1970.

36 Eggleston, J. F., and Kerr, J. F., *Studies in Assessment*. English Universities Press, 1969.

37 Morrison, A., and McIntyre, D., *Teachers and Teaching*. Penguin, 1969, p. 56.

38 Jecker, J. D., Maccoby, N., and Breitrose, H. S., 'Improving accuracy in interpreting non-verbal cues of comprehension', in *Psychology in the Schools*, 2, 1965, pp. 239-44.

39 Shapiro, D., and Schwartz, G. E., 'Psychophysiological contributions to social psychology', *Ann. Rev. Psychol.*, 21, 1970, pp. 87-112.

40 Fogelman, K. R., *Piagetian Tests for the Primary School*. Slough, Bucks., National Foundation for Educational Research, 1970.

41 Piaget, J., and Inhelder, B., in Fraisse, P., and Piaget, J. (ed.), *Experimental Psychology: Its Scope and Method, Vol. VII, Intelligence*. Routledge and Kegan Paul, 1969, pp. 196-202.

42 Sigel, I. E., and Hooper, F. H. (ed.), *Logical Thinking in Children*. New York, Holt, 1968.

43 *Ibid.*, pp. 423-34.

44 Thouless, R. H., *Map of Educational Research*. Slough, Bucks., National Foundation for Educational Research, 1969, p. 288.

45 Stephens, J. M., *The Process of Schooling*. New York, Holt, 1967, ch. 7.

46 Campbell, D. T., and Stanley, J. C., 'Experimental and quasi-experimental designs for research on teaching', in Gage, N. L. (ed.), *Handbook of Research on Teaching*. Chicago, Ill., Rand McNally, 1963.

47 *Ibid.*, p. 173.

48 *Ibid.*, p. 173.

49 *Ibid.*, p. 172.

50 Kersh, B. Y., and Wittrock, M. C., 'Learning by discovery: an interpretation of recent research', in *Journal of Teacher Education, 13*, 1962, pp. 461-8, reprinted in De Cecco, J. P. (ed.), *The Psychology of Language, Thought, and Instruction*. New York, Holt, 1967.

51 Hilgard, E. R., *Theories of Learning*. New York, Appleton-Century-Crofts, 2nd edition, 1956, pp. 485-7.

52 Hilgard, E. R., and Bower, G. H., *Theories of Learning*. New York, Appleton-Century-Crofts, 3rd edition, 1966, pp. 562-4; p. vii shows the primary author of the passage was E. R. Hilgard.

53 Hannam, C., Smyth, P., and Stephenson, N., *Young Teachers and Reluctant Learners*. Penguin, 1971.

54 Allen, D. W., and Ryan, K. A., *Microteaching*. Reading, Mass., Addison-Wesley, 1969.

55 Stones, E., and Anderson, D., *Objectives and the Teaching of Educational Psychology*. Birmingham University School of Education, 1970.

56 *Ibid.*, Appendices, p. ix.
57 *Ibid.*, Appendices, p. x.
58 *Ibid.*, p. 126.
59 Thouless, R. H., *op. cit.*, pp. 38, 291.
60 Robinson, P., in Burgess, T. (ed.), *Dear Lord James: a Critique of Teacher Education*. Penguin, 1971, p. 53.
61 Renshaw, P., in Burgess, T., *op. cit.*, p. 85.
62 Robinson, E., in Burgess, T., *op. cit.*, p. 142.
63 *Teaching Educational Psychology in Training Colleges.* The British Psychological Society, London, and The Association of Teachers in Colleges and Departments of Education, 1962.
64 Gagné, R. M., *The Conditions of Learning.* New York, Holt, 1970.
65 James, W., *Talks to Teachers on Psychology and to Students on Some of Life's Ideals.* Longmans, 1904, pp. 7-8.

Sociology of Education

Gerald Bernbaum

Of all contenders for their discipline's inclusion in the curricula
of institutions of higher education, sociologists should be the
least surprised about the ideological struggle in which they
have to engage in order for their justifications to gain acceptance. Those sociologists who are now beginning to study the
social context of the transmission of knowledge, and the way
in which forms of knowledge can be related to different types
of social control, emphasise the manner in which new knowledge can be used in altering established systems of authority.
As a result, those who exercise power and authority under the
existing arrangements might resist curriculum innovations
which they will see as threatening the status, prestige, rewards
and opportunities open to them under the prevailing structure.
Sociologists have themselves[1] drawn attention to the struggle
to introduce natural sciences into the school curriculum over a
century ago. And Professor Neustadt, by quoting Dr Arnold's
plea that rather than have the physical sciences 'the principal
thing in my son's mind, I would gladly have him think that
the sun went round the earth and that the stars were so many
spangles set in the bright blue firmament',[2] has reminded us
of the passion of those who defended the traditional classical
curriculum. Shortly after the natural sciences had established
their tentative grip on schools, English and literary studies
had, in their turn, to be strongly justified by those who wished
to bring them into the everyday school experience of the
majority of children. More recently, the whole structure of

tertiary education has been radically altered, in part at least, to enable more modern, technological, science-based subjects to be made available to students. The massive and continuing debate surrounding the expansion of higher education, and the arguments over the introduction of new, more applied subjects both inside and outside the universities, should serve as a useful reminder to sociologists that they are not alone in combating the interests and ideologies which derive from the established institutional and pedagogic arrangements in the educational system.

Social scientific perspectives on curriculum change serve to warn us how difficult it is to describe and explain the circumstances and conditions under which a new discipline will 'take' in an educational system and also draw our attention to the vital but complex processes which serve to diffuse new ideas and practices.[3] To undertake the kind of enquiry necessary to demonstrate both the descriptive and causal aspects of the growth of sociology as a teaching and research subject during the last decade is well beyond the scope of the present discussion. What can reasonably be asserted, however, is that sociologists, like the fervent proponents of all new disciplines, have enthusiastically made their case, and provide would-be doubters with the kinds of ideological justifications likely to soften the guardians of the conscience of liberal education, to appeal to the ruthless advocates of the scientific method, and also to attract students whose notions of what actually to expect are likely to be exceedingly vague and ill-formed.

The form of argument utilised by the sociologist-advocate is barely distinguishable from that used by those who expound the virtues of most other subjects. In essence, justifications are of two kinds, public good and private gain, though these need not be mutually exclusive. Thus, arguments are developed to recommend certain academic disciplines on the grounds that their pursuit will contribute to national well-being, albeit in terms of economic growth or public health. Other subjects, however, cannot lay claim to such manifest and collective benefits; for these the justifications are more private. The study is deemed to be valuable for its own sake, for the contribution it will make to personal development and awareness.

Now, as has already been proposed, the ideologies underlying particular disciplines might be very important in helping to establish a developing subject in the curriculum. Once established, moreover, a subject will probably benefit from the kind of justifications for its pursuit which enable it to attract resources, recruit students, impress the uninitiated and enhance the identity and self-concepts of its practitioners. It may be expected, therefore, that natural scientists should emphasise the importance of their work to the growth of the economy through their association with progress in technology and applied science, or that students of literature should propose the advantages of their subject in terms of the increased insight and sensitivity which it develops. What might be regarded as surprising, however, is that sociologists should so unselfconsciously elaborate the benefits of their own activities.

It might be regarded as surprising precisely because part of the sociologist's activity has been directed to questioning the validity of the simple relationships implied in the above justifications, or at least pointing out the complexities inherent in the causal links proposed, and emphasising the immense methodological problems involved in validating assertions which make simple assumptions about relationships when a whole variety of complex factors intervene with the passing of time. Thus, recent sociological enquiry has raised doubts about relationships which have been constantly reiterated in the past few years. Doubts have now been cast, for example, upon the contribution of education to economic growth,[4] and also upon its effect upon rates of upward social mobility in a society.[5] Similarly, the work undertaken on the impact of television programmes, even educational programmes, upon the audience, has shown that the effects may not always be what the producers intended,[6] and that there are many problems in making assertions about the effects of television. By extension, such findings should make sociologists, at least, wary of sweeping and unexamined claims for the contribution of any particular discipline to bring about radical change in an individual's personality, attitudes, and orientations upon life. If the sociologists have been made wary, however, they have, by and large, carefully concealed it, and there are many statements of the contribution which the study of sociology can make not only to the general education of students, but also to the special training of teachers.

The present discussion clearly necessitates a presentation of the claims which sociologists have made for their subject. In consideration of them, however, it is well to remember that the practitioners of all disciplines, especially new ones struggling for resources, time, and space, are likely to try to make their demands seem plausible to a wider public. If the advantages to be gained by the study of sociology are accepted as potential, then serious attention can be given to the contextual and peda-gogic problems of the transmission of the knowledge and its impact upon students. Finally, it should be noted that socio-logists choose to describe the beneficial effect of their discipline. There are critics, both in and out of higher education, who are convinced of the deleterious, almost sinful, effects which the study of sociology has upon students. They, too, might benefit from developing a respect for evidence and the methods by which it is collected. There is none which supports their pessimistic, and occasionally outrageous, assertions. Perhaps, after all, it could be argued that both sociologists and their enemies might benefit from a statement of the potential ad-vantages to be gained from pursuit of the new discipline.

Many of the virtues claimed for sociology are related to the benefits to be gained from a liberal education. Thus Bierstedt argues that sociology, like all the liberal arts, 'liberates the student from the provincialisms of time, place, and circum-stance'.[7] One of the great disadvantages of those who have not experienced the benefits of education is their parochialism, their attachment to the limited context of their own experience. Most of mankind rarely escape from the primitive but power-ful loyalties of their initial culture. For the uneducated the initial culture tends to be the permanent culture. And this provincialism, it should be noted, is not confined to rural or non-industrial societies. In the general sense in which 'parochialism' and 'provincialism' are being used here, some of the most provincial of the world's citizens are to be found in the largest, and apparently most sophisticated, conurbations.

It is commonplace to argue that travel might remove some of the restrictions embodied in an uneducated localism. It is not, however, sufficiently emphasised that it is possible to travel in time as well as space. Indeed, history can free us from the limitations of time and space by offering us an understanding of other places and other times. It is possible that sociology can do more than this. The historian might readily shake free the bonds imposed by his own culture only to become shackled by another. The sociologist, on the other hand, attempts to transcend all times, places and circumstances in his effort to elucidate the general principles that characterise human societies, societies which might be large or small, underdeveloped or advanced industrial, ancient or modern. In this sense, by moving from the particular and the concrete to the general and the abstract, the sociological liberation is essentially the liberation of science. We are all beset by groups which claim our loyalty – whether to race, religion, neighbourhood, or nation – and, as Bierstedt reminds us, 'in a world beset by provincialisms, by the ethnocentrisms of culture and temporocentrisms of era, period and century . . . sociology helps us to free ourselves from these particularistic controls and to learn to see a more universal society and a single human race. To see the eternal in the passing present, the universal in the particular fact, and the abstract in the concrete event – these are among the gifts of a liberal education.'[8]

It seems, therefore, that sociology is a worthwhile subject when considered in the light of the traditionally stated objectives for the experience of higher education. In this context it must be good for students, and perhaps especially those about to become teachers, to be brought to realise that there are other races and regions, classes and religions, neighbourhoods and nations, conceptions of the desirable and definitions of wrong.

Through the study of sociology the student has the opportunity to shed the particularism of his own experience, and to
enlarge that experience by the systematic examination of other
societies. Like both history and literature, it is not unreasonable
to hope that this might be a liberating activity for those who
undertake it.

The second of the educational advantages claimed for sociology is that it introduces the student to the nature and function
of logic and scientific method. Even a preliminary course in
sociology can introduce the student to the processes of abstrac-
tion and generalisation, and to the procedures involved in
induction from a concrete fact to an abstract principle. The
concepts of sociology – culture, norm, status, power, rôle,
institution – are not understood by immediate experience.
They represent an order of understanding beyond the pheno-
menal world in which the student has gained his direct experience. By studying sociology, therefore, the student has the
opportunity to understand the logical arrangements of class
inclusion, class identification and class membership, and also to
translate this experience in forms of concepts which are capable
of logical manipulation and inference. Such an understanding
should encourage in the student a concern for the nature and
character of definition and the rules of measurement. It is
possible to argue that sociology is almost unique in these qualities. In the humanities the scientific method traditionally plays
no part and in the sciences it is readily taken for granted; in
sociology, however, methodological questions are vital and
become matters of overt significance.

Sociologists are concerned with the patterns, regularities
and recurring configurations which exist in societies, and the
student is encouraged to look behind appearances and to attempt
to see the structure that constitutes an order. It cannot be
pretended that this is an easy task, but the very difficulty of
it has encouraged sociologists to acquire a methodological
sophistication that is not readily apparent elsewhere. Bierstedt
is confident that this concern with the logic of enquiry is a
vital feature of contemporary sociology, for he is sceptical of

the contributions made in this respect by either modern science or modern philosophy. He claims: 'It is in the social sciences, in our century at least, and especially in sociology, where men confront major methodological issues, and it is sociologists in consequence who acquire the kind of philosophical sophistication that no longer accompanies these other enquiries.'[9] It is possible to argue, therefore, that sociology offers a twofold advantage to its students. Firstly, there is that sense of order which it is the function of knowledge to impose upon the universe, and secondly, the experience of the logical processes involved in achieving it.

This is not all, however, for in so far as there is any validity in Snow's description of two cultures[10] then sociology clearly participates in both. It shares its subject matter with the humanities and its method with the sciences. Hurd has indicated, as a result of his own work with sixth forms, that 'Sir Charles Snow's suggestion that sociology genuinely speaks from one culture to another, thus creating a middle ground between the two cultures, was borne out'.[11] And Professor Bottomore has argued that 'sociology makes us aware of the wealth and diversity of human life. It is, or should be, the centrepiece of modern humane studies and a bridge between science and the humanities.'[12]

There is a case, therefore, for teaching sociology to students as part of their general education. Even those who will never go on to become professional sociologists should have the opportunity, at least, to profit from acquaintance with a liberal tradition and a liberalising influence. Obviously, student teachers are unlikely to develop into fully active sociologists, but the beneficial claims made for sociology might nevertheless be said to be relevant to them.

The relevance of sociology to teachers must be judged in terms of the benefits it can offer to those who work in the field of education. Neal Gross has proposed[13] that sociology is capable of making three significant contributions to educational theorists and practitioners. Firstly, it describes the impact of the external social system on the total educational process. Secondly,

G

it provides systematic analyses of the school as a major institution in society. Thirdly, it brings sociological theory and
method to bear on social interaction in the classroom setting.
Yet such a contribution will be scientific in method and will
produce data of an empirical kind. Paradoxically, its value to
the intending teacher will be in the challenge it provides
to the normative climate which determines his professional
socialisation.

In a stimulating fashion Marvin Bressler has described what
he calls the conventional wisdom of education.[14] He claims
that this normative climate in which the educationist works is
characterised by three basic propositions. First, formal education should develop cognitive skills, but this task does not
exhaust its responsibilities. The school must train young people
in all areas that crucially affect rôle performance. Second,
social change can be controlled by the application of disciplined intelligence. The educational process is the only alternative to social stagnation or revolutionary violence. It is the
duty of education to preside over gradualistic change toward
a more perfect expansion of the democratic tradition. Third,
all young people are capable of individual growth, and when
proper provisions are made for individual differences they can
all benefit from education at some level. If there is any validity
in Bressler's characterisation then it should be clear that the
study of sociology and the sociology of education present
some sort of challenge to the educationist. Indeed, Donald
Hansen has actually given us an essay on the subject entitled
'The Uncomfortable Relation of Sociology and Education'.[15]

The main points of the arguments developed by both Bressler
and Hansen is that the ideology or conventional wisdom of
education do not readily encourage free, scientific enquiry, as
they manifest the characteristics of dogma and faith. In
Bressler's own words, 'in the conventional wisdom of education truth and wish are one'.[16] A scientific study of social
relationships, therefore, such as is represented by sociology,
may easily be translated into the presentation of data which
might challenge faith and dogma, whilst the statement of

intellectual reservations and qualifications might be the occasion of accusatory outrage of the kind usually reserved for
heresy rather than doubt. One consequence of this is that what
is regarded as evidence by educationists is frequently an in-
substantial and vague selection of information designed to
support a stated point of view. As Amitai Etzioni bitingly
remarks of Silberman's *Crisis in the Classroom*, 'Ideas fly cheaply,
evidence is hard to muster.'[17]

The situation is exacerbated by the traditional mode of
recruitment into institutions for the training of teachers. The
very great majority of college of education staff are recruited
directly from the schools after years of schoolteaching experience. Any attempt to modify these arrangements usually
brings strong protests, especially from the teachers' unions
who have urged that no one should be appointed to a college
of education post without at least five years schoolteaching
experience. Two consequences have followed from this.
Firstly, it is extremely difficult for the educationist to develop
a serious grounding in the basic requirements of educational
research. The normal career line hardly allows for it. In teacher
training, therefore, those subjects which are not widely taught
in the schools, like sociology, psychology and philosophy, are
likely to be entrusted to lecturers who were appointed primarily because of their schoolteaching experience in fields other
than these core disciplines. Yet educational research and analysis
is likely to be conducted and enlarged in terms of these disciplines. It is not without reason that the last major specialist
report on the colleges of education noted that they 'have never
ranked in the public mind as institutions which have a duty as
regards the promotion of research and investigation in the
field of education'.[18] As the career of the educationist offers
him little opportunity to acquire the specialised knowledge
of the foundation disciplines and only perfunctory training in
the logic and techniques of enquiry, he is unlikely to excel in
social, psychological, or philosophical investigation even if he
wished to do so. The second consequence of the emphasis
given to practical experience in teacher education is that those

engaged in it are likely to have an action orientation. The lecturer's own appointment has been made on the basis of his presumed expertise in teaching; it is difficult, therefore, for him to appear less enthusiastic about his own teaching than he is proposing his students be about theirs. The degree of effort and energy required for the activity of teaching necessarily involves a lessening of the energy which the lecturer can give to other things, such as research. Furthermore the action and experiential orientation of education staff might well lead them to be impatient with the whole business of research which is informed by the perspectives and methods of the social sciences. Such research is likely to be conducted over a number of years, the results may be so hedged with qualifications that no clear and immediate policy recommendations can be made, or even when they can, there is likely to be a time lapse between the finding and its incorporation into practice.

Moreover, the uncomfortable relationship of sociology and education can be explained not only by the differing ideologies and values which underly the two areas, but also by certain features of the structure and organisation of the colleges of education. Though in recent years the size of colleges has grown, the growth has been uneven and its impact has not been universally felt. Relative to other institutions of higher education many colleges of education are still small, and the observations of the McNair Committee as long ago as 1944 are probably even more true today: 'the small size of many colleges means that one lecturer must play many rôles and many specialists are naturally unwilling to do this or to learn to do it'.[19] Moreover, it must be recognised that in many cases this lack of specialisation is made a virtue. The generalist and eclectic nature of education courses becomes justified on ideological grounds associated with the advantages of breaking down subject barriers and the benefits of interdisciplinary enquiry. As it is precisely these developments which are being recommended in the schools, it is almost impossible for education lecturers not to seem to be willing to break down the apparently restricting barriers in their own teaching.

It is argued, therefore, that in so far as the sociology of education is part of the overall responsibility of the department of education in the colleges it is likely to experience that degree of difficulty which both Hansen and Bressler have described in the United States, and it is likely that the whole development of the field of enquiry will be retarded by the synthetic, non-specialist, practical and action orientation which characterises much of the work in colleges. In a real sense the introduction of sociology challenges many of the unexamined assumptions upon which the work of the colleges rests.

It must not be assumed, however, that the advent of sociology in the colleges necessarily heralds the adoption of totally new perspectives in teaching and research. Quite the reverse: given the existing structure of power, and network of ideologies described, then one possibility is that what passes as sociology in colleges and departments of education will itself become modified so that it is seen as presenting less of a challenge. That this might occur can be suggested by a brief examination of the introduction of two other disciplines into the field of education, philosophy and psychology.

Professor Peters has distinguished two types of philosophy which are institutionalised in the colleges of education.[20] Firstly, there is that concerned with principles of education which he sees as occupied with the cementation of values, the dispensing of wisdom about education. As Peters has written, 'this omnibus conception of his [the philosopher's] task is partly a relic of the old conception of the philosopher as a kind of oracle and partly due to an undifferentiated conception of educational studies which dies hard in some educational circles'.[21] Secondly, Peters points out how the dispensation of wisdom is often reinforced with 'supports from what the great educators of the past have said about it . . . a Cook's tour of thinkers from Plato to Dewey'.[22] Little wonder that Peters claims that when philosophers look at what goes on in colleges of education they are usually appalled at what they find.

Now it is interesting to analyse the fate of psychology as it

G*

was introduced into the colleges of education. In many ways, making due allowance for the differences in the nature of the subjects, it seems to have suffered the same fate as philosophy as it has been accommodated to the prevailing structure and ideology of the colleges. The report of a joint working party of the British Psychological Society and the Association of Teachers in Colleges and Departments of Education has given us a picture of the place of psychology in the training colleges in 1959.[23] This report points out how in 'Training Colleges psychology had perforce to be taught by the "Master of Method" or the junior or infant "method" lecturer'. From the beginning, therefore, psychology was immersed in general courses in education and the appointment to college staffs of specialist psychologists hardly altered the situation. The joint report, for example, shows how difficult the colleges found it to estimate the amount of time spent on psychology because in 76 out of the 98 colleges who replied the psychological aspects of education were not separated from the study of aims, values, history, and philosophy. The enquiry also looked at examination questions in psychology which may be taken as a possible guide to what is considered significant, and an indication of the areas to which the student's attention must be drawn. Again, the ideological elements in the courses become immediately apparent, the concern with problems and practical experience being especially noticeable. As the authors of the report indicate, 'There were . . . relatively few questions on educational attainment of normal children but many on educational failure and remedial treatment . . . over three-quarters of the questions on adjustment were on the causes, diagnosis and treatment of maladjusted children. . . . On the whole, the approach appeared to be empirical rather than theoretical. The questions on learning, for example, seemed to be based on a knowledge of established classroom practice together with some of the more important experimental findings. Very few asked for general underlying theoretical principles about learning. . . . Again the questions on intelligence were almost wholly on the practical appreciation of tests in school.'[24]

Furthermore, the report shows the great deal of variation in the psychological qualifications of the staff concerned with the teaching of psychology. Thirty-nine per cent of those with the responsibility for teaching psychology had no formal qualification whatsoever.

Thus it can be seen that the traditional values of the training college system, particularly the emphasising of the pastoral element in teaching, along with structural features of the colleges, especally the position of the education department, have greatly affected the manner in which both philosophy and psychology have been taught to prospective teachers. There is evidence to suggest that similar processes are at work as sociology courses come into the colleges. Orville Brim, writing of the situation in the United States,[25] has shown that this might be a general and widespread problem. 'The fact is that much of what passes under the name of sociological training of educators is carried on by persons trained in education not sociology. One must recognise that unfortunately the materials presented are frequently pseudosociology, consisting of moralistic and philosophical content rather than research and theory. They may be variously termed, such as social stratification, community organisation, or the family, but they often turn out to be sociology in name only.'

Despite many recent changes in the colleges it is doubtful whether the difficulties arising from what William Taylor has called the romanticism[26] of the colleges have greatly altered. Certainly the position of the education department itself within the college has not been seriously questioned in official circles. The recent report on the government of colleges of education (the Weaver Report) emphasises the responsibility of the education department in a college when it asserts 'that the professional preparation of teachers should be related as closely as possible to the demands that will be made on them in the classroom',[27] while in 1957 a report by the Inspectorate insisted that 'any fragmentation of the course of training tends to frustrate the ablest students and bewilder the weakest'.[28]

The essentially synthetic approach of the education department and its denial of specialisation or differentiation in academic work is especially manifest in a publication entitled *The Work of the Training Colleges* issued in 1963 by the Department of Education and Science.[29] This pamphlet is meant as a guide to the work of the colleges, especially for those contemplating becoming members of staff. Significantly, it argues that 'a teacher in education will work as a member of a team, being particularly concerned with the educational problems of a particular age range of children'[30] and informs its readers that for entry to the staff of a college 'the only "must" is successful, relevant and substantial teaching experience'.[31]

The authors of the pamphlet claim that education should be placed 'in the centre of all the studies undertaken in the college',[32] but go on to indicate that this does not necessarily involve rigorous study but rather an acquisition of certain attributes of a normative character. It is said that the students 'have to develop an understanding of, rather than knowledge about, children and themselves. They have to acquire attitudes towards, rather than mere accomplishments in, their work as teachers',[33] and it appears that 'the strength of the education course lies in the study of the growth of children from birth to adulthood . . . Thus from studies of individual children or small groups of children, in and out of school, the students lay the foundations of their understanding.'[34] Little wonder that the only specialism the education lecturer needs is 'in understanding children and also in human relations',[35] especially when it appears that 'though the main lectures on any subject will be given by a lecturer specially qualified *or interested in* it, all the other members of the department will be expected to take part in less formal teaching, seminars or discussions designed to emphasise and *illustrate from experience* the points made by the lecturer' (my italics).[36]

These lengthy quotations clearly illustrate many of the features associated with the colleges which have already been described. It should be remembered that the document from which they are drawn is fairly recent and that it is designed to encourage staff to become college lecturers by providing them with information about the nature of their tasks. Yet it shows quite clearly an ambiguous attitude towards academic work. The work of the education lecturer is essentially all-purpose, non-specialist. Its starting point is the child, and his relationships, but nowhere is there any explicit recognition that such things can be studied in a scientific fashion. Instead there is great emphasis placed on the value of experience and on the importance of a sort of affective insight and relationship which is never clearly specified. It is not surprising, therefore, to find that the structural features of the colleges and their associated ideologies have affected the nature and content of the sociology of education as it has been introduced into the colleges.

Concern over the problems associated with the beginnings of sociology in the colleges is clearly shown in articles appearing in the journal *Education for Teaching*, the publication of the body which represents college of education staff. The articles, appearing over the last ten years or so, have regularly discussed the principles involved in teaching sociology in the colleges and given representative examples of syllabuses. In 1961 William Taylor, in an article designed to present a syllabus of sociology of education for the colleges, made the distinction between 'educational sociology' and the 'sociology of education', the latter being more rigorous and more likely to satisfy the standards of the professional sociologists. He warned that there is 'little point in calling part of a college of education course "sociological" when in fact the topics considered would not be recognised by most sociologists as being within their legitimate province'.[37] There is evidence, however, that Taylor's warnings have not been heeded. Recent articles have found advocates of sociology among those who seem to have little clear understanding of the nature of the subject and who continue to support it for reasons mostly associated with the special insights that the teacher is supposed to require for handling working-class children, or for the contribution it can make to the overall 'efficiency' of the educational system. Thus

Craft has written in an article actually entitled 'Why Sociology for Teachers?' that '. . . the gap in understanding between working-class parents and the average teacher are now familiar aspects of educational sociology, and examples perhaps of what the teacher needs to know'.[38] In the same journal in February 1966 Shaw claims that 'a sociology of education course for teachers will set out to explain how influences from the wider society affect schools . . . and the capacity of their pupils to profit from the courses offered'.[39] In the same issue Otley indicates his view that a course in sociology at a college of education '. . . needs to be *oriented* towards topics which are of some immediate utility and relevance to intending teachers',[40] and goes on to assert that 'subjects like the property and power structure of modern Britain, the nature of legal and political institutions and religious phenomena, for instance, are not at all suitable for the ordinary college student'.[41]

Moreover, MacGuire found in her investigation of the position of sociology in the colleges in 1961[42] that the situation was one which could not be considered satisfactory. She showed that the development of sociology faced the problems associated with the growth of academic work in the colleges. MacGuire's enquiry was conducted amongst 103 training colleges and 19 university departments of education. Amongst the colleges she had replies from 73 (46 per cent) and her data relate to these colleges only. Sixty-three of the colleges did not run specific courses in sociology while 10 claimed to run specific courses in some aspect of sociology. Twenty-five of the colleges included sociological topics in other courses, the most popular place being the principles of education courses, though four colleges claimed to be teaching some sociology in home management courses and three in health education. Only two of the colleges which taught sociology in 'other courses' had staff with graduate qualifications in sociology, and of the 10 colleges which taught sociology only six had staff with any qualification in sociology.

However, it is when the topics covered are looked at that it becomes possible to see most clearly how the prevailing structure and ideology of the colleges are reflected in a problem-oriented approach emphasising the 'difficult' areas of education and what might be called a 'cultural' concern. Popular elements in the sociology courses studied by MacGuire were: the agencies which deal with children (for example, the probation service, child guidance); the social groups, relevant to the child, of family and school, street, neighbourhood; social problems (for example, delinquency, adolescence, leisure and the effects of the mass media). Little wonder that MacGuire could point out that 'the study of social class was not specifically mentioned nor was the assessment of research data'.[43]

It seems, therefore, that as in the case of philosophy and psychology, the beginning of sociology in the colleges has been marked by the adoption of a highly selective view of the subject, a view which is least likely to challenge the existing ideological positions there. It is possible to explain, therefore, why much of the sociology of education that is taught is problem oriented, and why so much of what frequently appears in sociology of education courses is more accurately dealt with under the heading of social work. Similarly it can be seen why the methods of group dynamics are acceptable as a form of social science in the colleges. These are the areas which challenge the ideology of education least – that is to say, the sociologist's perspectives may only be welcomed when they deal with 'critical' educational issues and can obviously be seen to proceed from a humane set of values, or, perhaps, when they contain substantive findings which either implicitly or explicitly offer concrete proposals for action. Thus, the attention given to such topics as social problems, disadvantaged children, deviancy and the like is perfectly explicable. In this way, also, it is possible for the educationist to maintain his hostility to parts of sociology which can be dismissed as not relevant or too technical. A recent president of the N.U.T. has argued that the teachers 'have felt that such people (sociologists and psychologists) do not know the problems of the classroom. They need to be reassured that many who are concerned in research have been teachers and know the problems of the classroom. They need to be able to see that the results of the research can be written in such a way that the understanding of the teacher's problem is not excluded in the profusion of evidence and conclusions...'As Bressler has remarked, 'for the educationist science is an honoured symbol, but experience becomes the actual basis for knowledge'.[44]

The way that sociology of education has become institutionalised in colleges of education should serve as a salutary and cautionary warning to all who hope for too much from the introduction of the sociological perspective. Nevertheless, it is still possible to reflect on the potential advantages of education students being given a thoroughgoing course in sociology and to describe some of the features which might characterise such a course.

A systematic study of the sociology of education could enlarge and enhance the usual perspectives adopted by educationists by increasing the range of variables and concepts manifest in their approach. Teachers and students of education who come to look at schools have already been sensitised by the values, norms, ideologies, life styles and modes of behaviour of their own particular social groups. They have already been exposed to a powerful 'folk' sociology. Yet the convictions, beliefs and attitudes embodied in such a sociology may not stand up to scientific examination. At the same time, it should be recognised that to embark on the scientific study of society might present difficult emotional problems to young people. The discussion of social phenomena such as 'class', 'power', 'authority', 'social control', 'conflict', all of which might be relevant to a scientific examination of schools and the educational process, is likely to represent a challenging experience. There is a sense, therefore, in which a student of sociology has to undergo what Professor Neustadt has described as a process 'of unlearning . . . mythological conceptions about the nature of social institutions or the conventional ranking of social groups and of individuals which he usually accepts because he has been brought up with them without any awareness that one can subject them to a critical examination. Above all, he has to unlearn the deep rooted habit of evaluating these phenomena in terms of criteria derived from estimations of right and wrong or references to wickedness or virtue.'[45] In this way teachers could come to a greater understanding of the nature and significance of systematic group differences. Sociological perspectives can draw attention to the importance of institutional arrangements in the causation of individual strain and also specify the structured sources of individual differences. Furthermore, an important contribution of the sociology of education has been to identify and elaborate in quantitative terms those characteristics of a given population that encourage or prevent learning. It seems reasonable to argue that a teacher who is aware of such patterned differences should be more able to understand both the complexities of his task and the requirements of his pupils. He should also, because of his understanding of the social context of learning, be able to distance himself from the individualistic aspects of many parts of the conventional beliefs surrounding education. Success or failure, on the part of either teachers or pupils, can come to be seen in terms other than those of individual merit.

The educationist or prospective teacher could also benefit from the tough-mindedness implicit in the best scientific sociology, and in its corollary, the careful attention paid to problems of methodology and theory construction. Altogether the field of education lacks the disinterestedness which is part of the scientific perspective. As a discipline, sociology has a sense of complexity and a deliberate consciousness of the uncertainty implicit in current knowledge which militates against rigid adherence to fixed positions, especially those formed by untestable assertions. As Berger has noted, 'the first wisdom of sociology is this . . . things are not what they seem . . . social reality turns out to have many layers of meaning. The discovery of each new layer changes the perception of the whole.'[46]

Sociology, then, might enable the teachers to come to a different and, in a real sense, better understanding of their work for, as Burns has argued, 'the purpose of sociology is to

achieve an understanding of social behaviour and social institutions which is different from that current among the people
through whose conduct the institutions exist; an understanding
which is not merely different but new and better. The practice
of sociology is criticism. It exists to criticise claims about the
value of achievement and to question assumptions about the
meaning of conduct. It is the business of sociologists to conduct
a critical debate with the public about its equipment of social
institutions.'[47]

In these respects sociology may have a great deal to offer
education. Systematic sociological enquiry has already shown,
for example, that the Education Act of 1944, which was
designed to promote equality of educational opportunity,
actually did so in only a very limited fashion. And this was
not in any way due to maladministration or insincerity, but
simply that the variables that control educational opportunity
and educational achievement, like the occupational and family
structures and the social circumstances of the child, were not
conceived as affecting attainment in the ways and to the extent
which sociological investigation have now shown them to do.

As has already been argued, such uses of sociology might
be acceptable to educationists and teachers. But they must
remember that they should be prepared to accept the relevance
of the scientific method to the study of their own activities.
There are signs that when sociologists begin to examine, say,
the internal organisation of schools,[48] or aspects of the teaching
profession, their enquiries are not so welcome. Hostility to
scientific investigation of social phenomena should not worry
sociologists too greatly; they should be used to it. Aubert's
study[49] of the judiciary in Norway gave rise to violent reactions
amongst the legal profession when it was first published, precisely because the evidence showed that, in giving sentence,
judges appeared to be following a tacit code which contravened
the explicit code of equality before the law. Aubert demonstrated that the variation in sentencing behaviour correlated
extremely closely with the social class of the accused person.
Other studies have confirmed these findings, and now, as a

result of sociological enquiry, the social basis of sentencing policy is more openly and more accurately understood. In studies of educational opportunity also, the sociologist has shown how complex normative patterns might greatly affect public principles of action, and in this way illuminated the working of an important social institution.

In education, hostility has already been demonstrated to studies which, for example, suggest that traditional institutional arrangements in a school might actually inhibit the learning and achievement of at least some of the pupils.[50] Scientific investigation, however, should also pose problems to those who advocate educational change on ideological grounds. There is increasing evidence which suggests that the benefits to be derived from non-streaming are not necessarily of the kind, quantitatively or qualitatively, that those who have most frequently advocated the changes supposed. This evidence suggests that the academic achievement of working-class pupils in the unstreamed situations is not markedly different from their performance in streamed classes, and that they still do less well than middle-class pupils.[51] Moreover, it is the sociologists who have shown that the transmission of knowledge occurs in a social context and that attempts to alter the curriculum or introduce new teaching methods must be seen in the context of the implications which they have for changing the social rôles of pupil and teacher,[52] or in the light of their significance for a new basis of social control and the problem of authority.[53] Sociological enquiry of this kind shows clearly the relevance of Popper's description of sociology as being concerned with the unanticipated consequences of human action. Sociology should make us aware of the unintended consequences implicit in *recommendations* to human action.

If it does this, sociology is likely to move into a position where it takes a sceptical view of prescriptions for educational change. This will not be a question of challenging the underlying humane values of those who propose reforms in education, but more a matter of examining the conditions which make for its success or failure. Those in education who distrust such an approach should remember that much of their best evidence for the attack on existing educational institutions and processes comes from the enquiries of sociologists. And they should also remind themselves that too much utopianism on the part of educators might be a major alienating factor amongst their pupils. The benefits of scientific sociology should serve to unite those who wish to change educational policy and institutions with those who appreciate that this can best be done on the basis of evidence rather than faith.

Those who have grand schemes for the reform of education, and through it the reform of society, would do well to remember what Spencer wrote a hundred years ago. His illustration provides a graphic justification for a science of society:

> You see that this wrought-iron plate is not quite flat; it sticks up a little here toward the left – 'cockles', as we say. How shall we flatten it? Obviously, you reply, by hitting down on the part that is prominent. Well, here is a hammer and I give the plate a blow as you advise. Harder, you say. Still no effect. Another stroke: well, there is one, and another, and another. The prominence remains, you see: the evil is as great as ever – greater, indeed. But this is not all. Look at the warp which the plate has got near the opposite edge. Where it was flat before it is now curved. A pretty bungle we have made of it. Instead of curing the original defect, we have produced a second. Had we asked an artisan practised in 'planishing', as it is called, he would have told us that no good was to be done, but only mischief, by hitting down on the projecting part. He would have taught us how to give variously-directed and specially-adjusted blows with a hammer elsewhere: so attacking the evil not by direct but by indirect actions. The required process is less simple than you thought. Even a sheet of metal is not to be successfully dealt with after those common sense methods in which you have so much confidence. What, then, shall we say about a society? . . . Is humanity more readily straightened than an iron plate?[54]

In conclusion, it is possible to consider the implications of this analysis in terms of what might be offered to students of the sociology of education. It should be clear from the discussion that the sociology of education is not a re-ordering of topics usually associated with 'social studies'. It is a vigorous and disciplined analysis of educational institutions, their changing forms, and of developments of the manifold inter-relationships between such institutions and the wider society, such an analysis being conducted in the light of sociological principles and methods of enquiry.

If this is the case, then it can be argued that the student of education or the prospective teacher requires an understanding of the four major socialising agencies: the family, the age group, school, and work. The student should be made aware of the importance of the nature and extent of inter-personal relationships in family life for the potential development of the child, and the way in which such relationships vary with the value system and social class position of the parents. Similarly, students should be encouraged to develop an understanding of peer group influence on both the social behaviour and academic achievement of pupils. Particularly relevant here are many sociological studies of adolescents and of students, studies which should serve the student not only by telling him about those whom he might teach, but also by throwing light on the ambiguities and strains inherent in his own position.

Obviously, a prospective teacher will require some understanding of schools as social forms: their development, their selective functions, their rituals and ceremonies. He will need to know about their mechanisms of social control and their authority relationships, their expressive and instrumental cultures. Particularly, in view of recent changes, students will require to be presented with some analysis of the inter-relations between curricula, social organisation and the social composition of the pupils.

Finally, the student will need knowledge of the occupational system and the economy, especially the way in which they relate to the educational system, and the mechanism which translate change in one to change in the other.

It is of course unreasonable to suppose that the study of the sociology of education will transform educational organisations or those who work in them. But the steady accumulation of data by publicly-stated methods, the modification and elaboration of theories which are capable of being scientifically tested and the creation of a mood which informs such approaches should enable us to move closer to a real, and hence more truthful, view of educational processes and educational institutions. It is to be hoped that educationists, at least, are not amongst those who regret this.

References

1 Hurd, G. E., *The Teaching of the Social Sciences in Secondary Schools, with special reference to the Teaching of Sociology*. M.A. Dissertation, University of Leicester, 1963.
2 Neustadt, I., *Teaching Sociology*. Leicester University Press, 1965, p. 5.
3 Rogers, E., *Diffusion of Innovations*. New York, Collier-Macmillan, 1965.
4 Hurd, G. E., and Johnson, T., 'Education and development', in *Sociological Review*, March 1967.
5 Blau, P. M., and Duncan, O. O., *The American Occupational Structure*. New York, John Wiley, 1967.
6 Halloran, J. D. (ed.), *The Effects of Television*. Panther Books, 1970.
7 Bierstedt, R., 'Sociology and general education', in Page, C. H. (ed.), *Sociology and Contemporary Education*. New York, Random House, 1963, p. 41.
8 *Ibid.*, p. 42.
9 *Ibid.*, p. 47.
10 Snow, C. P., *The Two Cultures and the Scientific Revolution*. Cambridge University Press, 1959.
11 Hurd, G. E., 'Sociology for sixth formers?', in *Educ. Rev.*, *17*, June 1965, pp. 209-10.
12 Bottomore, T., *Sociology*. Allen and Unwin, 1962, p. 23.
13 Gross, N., 'Some contributions of sociology to the field of education', in *Harv. Educ. Rev.*, *29*, Fall 1959, pp. 275-87.
14 Bressler, M., 'The conventional wisdom of education and sociology', in Page, C. H. (ed.), *Sociology and Contemporary Education*. New York,

Random House, 1963. I have drawn heavily on Bressler's stimulating essay.

15 Hansen, D. A., 'The uncomfortable relation of sociology and education', in Hansen, D. A., and Gerstl, J. E. (ed.), *On Education — Sociological Perspectives.* New York, John Wiley, 1967.
16 Bressler, M., *op. cit.*, p. 83.
17 Etzioni, A., in a review of Silberman, E., *Crisis in the Classroom.* See *Harv. Educ. Rev.*, *41*, 1, February 1971, p. 93.
18 *Teachers and Youth Leaders* (McNair Report). H.M.S.O., 1944, p. 71.
19 *Ibid.*, p. 73.
20 Peters, R. S., 'The philosophy of education', in Tibble, J. W. (ed.), *The Study of Education.* Routledge and Kegan Paul, 1965.
21 *Ibid.*, p. 64.
22 *Ibid.*, p. 64.
23 *Teaching Educational Psychology in Training Colleges.* British Psychological Society, London, 1962.
24 *Ibid.*, p. 21.
25 Brim, O. R., *Sociology and the Field of Education.* New York, Russell Sage Foundation, 1958, p. 75.
26 Taylor, W., *Society and the Education of Teachers.* Faber and Faber, 1969.
27 *The Government of Colleges of Education* (Weaver Report). H.M.S.O., 1966, p. 17.
28 *The Training of Teachers.* H.M.S.O., 1957, p. 14.
29 *The Work of the Training Colleges.* H.M.S.O., 1963
30 *Ibid.*, p. 5.
31 *Ibid.*, p. 5.
32 *Ibid.*, p. 12.
33 *Ibid.*, p. 12.
34 *Ibid.*, p. 12.
35 *Ibid.*, p. 15.
36 *Ibid.*, p. 14.
37 Taylor, W., 'The sociology of education in the training college', in *Education for Teaching*, February 1961, p. 46.
38 Craft, M., 'Why sociology for teachers?', in *Education for Teaching*, November 1963, p. 32.
39 Shaw, K. E., 'Why no sociology of schools', in *Education for Teaching*, February 1966, p. 61.
40 Otley, C. B., 'Sociology in the college of education', in *Education for Teaching*, February 1966, p. 57.
41 *Ibid.*, p. 57.
42 MacGuire, J. M., 'Sociology for teachers', in *Education for Teaching*, May 1963.

43 *Ibid.*, p. 17.
44 Bressler, M., *op cit.*, p. 91.
45 Neustadt, I., *op. cit.*, p. 11.
46 Berger, P. L., *Invitation to Sociology.* Penguin, 1966, p. 34.
47 Burns, T., 'Sociological explanation', in *Br. J. Sociol.*, *XVIII*, December 1967, pp. 36-7.
48 Hargreaves, D. H., *Social Relations in a Secondary School.* Routledge and Kegan Paul, 1967.
49 Aubert, V., *Sociology of Law.* Oslo, Institute for Social Research, 1964 (mimeographed).
50 Lacey, C., *Hightown Grammar: The School as a Social System.* Manchester University Press, 1970.
51 Barker-Lunn, J. C., *Streaming in the Primary School.* Slough, Bucks., National Foundation for Educational Research, 1970.
52 Musgrove, F., 'The contribution of sociology to the study of the curriculum', in Kerr, J. F. (ed.), *Changing the Curriculum.* University of London Press, 1968.
53 Bernstein, B., 'On the classification and framing of educational knowledge', in Young, M. (ed.), *Knowledge and Control.* New York, Collier-Macmillan, 1971.
54 Spencer, H., *The Study of Sociology.* New York, 1875, pp. 270-1.

Index